C000058333

Dancing to the Beat
of the Drum

Dancing to the Beat
of the Drum

PAMELA NOMVETE

Copyright © 2019 by Pamela Nomvete.

All rights reserved. No part of this publication may be reproduced, distributed, or transmitted in any form or by any means, including photocopying, recording, or other electronic or mechanical methods, without the prior written permission of the author, except in the case of brief quotations embodied in critical reviews and certain other noncommercial uses permitted by copyright law.

Printed in the United States of America
ISBN 978-1-733289-67-2 (sc)
ISBN 978-1-733289-66-5 (e)

Autobiography

2019 | 08 | 20

Pamela Nomvete Books

Contents

Dedication

This book is dedicated to my beloved parents who always taught me that "failure" is never an option. To my siblings who have always come through for me whatever differences we may have had.

To Daisaku Ikeda my mentor without whom I would never have had the courage to write a book and who encourages me always to push past my limitations.

The sangomas say that when it is time to connect with your true calling, your true self, you must "dance to the beat of the drum".

In 1994 I had gone to South Africa to vote and ended up staying there for fourteen years.

July 2010, while working at the National Theatre in London, I decided to return to Johannesburg, having left three years earlier with a view never to return.

Never to return . . .

"Why never to return?" I ask myself.

The reasons:
1. A failed marriage
2. A failed career
3. Total failure in my relationship with my homeland

All of which led me to decide to skulk back to England, my spiritual and professional home, to get some perspective on the situation. The "situation" was my life!

Let's start at the beginning, shall we? Or is it more like somewhere in the middle?

YOUNG AND RESTLESS

1

1994. South Africa is voting. In the famous words of Dr Martin Luther King Jr: "Free at last, free at last, thank God almighty, free at last."

Those words rang in my ears as the whole world awaited the much-anticipated first free elections held in South Africa. Naturally, having watched my parents dedicate their whole lives to this day, I was on a plane in April 1994 to Johannesburg, so I could vote. This was my parents' vision made manifest. With the liberation of South Africa came the liberation of the African continent.

My father, Bax Dale Nomvete, a brilliant young South African, son of a priest, one Fletcher Nomvete, was one of the first black South Africans to be accepted at Cape Town University in the early 1950s. He married Corah Sibongile Kumalo, the daughter of Chief Walter Kumalo of Ladysmith, Natal. Excelling in his studies, he was offered a scholarship at Manchester University. At the time, my eldest sister had just been born. My maternal grandmother suggested my mother leave for Manchester with my father and prepare a home for the baby. My sister would follow when the time was right. After much painful deliberation, this plan was agreed upon by the three of them. Pretty straightforward and feasible in an ideal world.

Whilst at the university, my father gave many talks on the situation in South Africa, and to the horror of both my parents the apartheid government declared my parents exiled. The government threatened them, telling them that if they continued to tell the truth about South Africa they would never see their child again. The apartheid government destroyed my sister's birth certificate, and my parents fought for five years to get their child out of apartheid hell and to safety in their arms in the United Kingdom.

The irony in all of this was that a Conservative government was in power in the UK at the time and some Quaker friends of my parents encouraged them to petition the government to order the release of my sister on humanitarian grounds. So they did, and the Conservative government of Great Britain so ordered.

Let us just think about that for a second. To bring my sister out of the land of her birth and into exile my parents appealed to a government filled with individuals who really were not that interested in having more rejected Africans populating their small island. And this guaranteed her safety.

You can imagine the kind of trauma this caused in my family. I am not sure how many wounds have had to be healed because of it, but having lived the life I have led, having been given the opportunities I have had, I am proud of my parents and my sister for overcoming what could have destroyed my family forever. And I mean forever because this kind of trauma tends to bleed into generation after generation after generation. Someone has to stop that flow of contaminated blood, and in my family, in my opinion, they did.

Where did this leave me? As a child born in exile, with no real relationship with South Africa, negative or positive. I grew up calling myself a South African because my parents managed to help me understand that I had every right to claim my heritage. But the question still remained: Was I a South African?

I know I am an African, even though I grew up in an international community. Let me explain.

I was born in Addis Ababa, Ethiopia.

Africa Hall, in Addis Ababa, was my father's workplace.

Africa Hall was the place that housed the economic commission for the Africa division of the United Nations, and my father was the director.

I saw the whole continent roll in and out of there. Somehow, under that majestic umbrella of Africa Hall, African unity seemed possible.

Hell, people were speaking Amharic, Yoruba, Swahili, Xhosa, Zulu and on and on.

The downside of this multiculturalism was that it was just easier for my sister, Sheila—who had also been born in Ethiopia—and me to speak English. Yes, you guessed it; we never learned any of our home languages. Out of the four children born of Bax and Corah Nomvete, the eldest, Quezi, was the only one of us born in South Africa, and she left at the age of five when, as you have learned, the British government of the time ordered her release on "humanitarian" grounds. But not knowing my home tongue was never a hindrance in this idyllic world of African unity, where it was understood that English was the language we all spoke.

Idyllic. That is definitely how I would describe my childhood. Idyllic.

Here we were witness to energetic, colourful gatherings my parents hosted over and over again. We would creep out of our bedrooms in our pyjamas and find a spot where we were hidden so we could watch the dynamic individuals sweep in and out of our house.

Some were future leaders of countries, some were to lead and die for justice, some were to become recognised as world-class artists—the likes of Chris Hani, Kofi Anan and Miriam Makeba—and all the time my mother and father chanted, "Unity, unity, unity." Unity meant the emancipation of the individual that would lead to the emancipation of communities, countries and, eventually, the continent.

These were high-powered individuals that were working to build the richest continent in the world, but our parents never stopped being our parents.

Every year, one of the gatherings was, of course, to celebrate New Year. At five to midnight, my dad would come and find us, open the car doors in the garage, and, on the dot of midnight, would tell us to honk that car horn. We did it loudly and with such abandon. I loved that moment and as a result New Year's Eve is still my favourite time of year.

All these colourful folks were just "uncle" and "auntie" to us. Our parents' dream. The most natural thing in the world.

Idyllic. That is how I would describe my childhood.

Life, as we all know, is never static. We happily travelled from country to country with our parents. One of the countries we lived in was Zambia. Still, the African heroes graced our home, even more frequently, in fact, as we were so very close to "home" and in the heart of the African countries that had pledged to shelter South African freedom fighters who'd had to flee the land of their birth.

It was here I met Chris Hani. Legend. News of his death is something that marred my young life and still leaves a very bitter taste in my mouth.

I wonder what freedom in South Africa would have looked like had he lived.

Freedom fighters frequented our house time and time again to hear my father share his economic vision for Africa. A united Africa. Long before the European Union was being constructed, my father had written document after document detailing how an African Union could work. He had written those documents in the 1960s, and now in the '70s he was attempting to bring his dream to fruition. He created an organisation called the Preferential Trade Area that succeeded in creating the first southern African traveller's cheques. We could, for the first time, travel from Zambia to Zimbabwe on one currency.

This brought a great deal of pressure on my father, who was ostracized over and over again as Western powers systematically turned African leaders against his plan. There were always threats on his life and I remember this as being one of the most painful times in our family's history.

Living in Zambia meant that we were within touching distance of "home", and yet we couldn't actually set foot there. In a strange way this added to my parents' frustrations. On a practical level it meant that my dad had to find alternative routes when flying to African countries that you would usually get to via Johannesburg. On a deeper level being so close to home and family without being able to see either was torture.

I was fortunate to meet my maternal grandmother before she died—they managed, after much discussion, to get her out to Botswana. Not long after that, she left this world. I remember feeling so grateful, as I watched my mother collapse with grief, that she had been able to reconnect with her mother one last time.

Finally, the powers that be, helped along by greedy, short-sighted African leaders, thwarted my father's African Union plan. Everything was frozen, and as a result Nomvete's dream of economic emancipation was hidden from the African people. It was locked away in some cupboard, no doubt, in some African court, or has been destroyed.

Here is a little gem to end this chapter. A young man by the name of Uncle Thabo frequented our house and would often babysit my sister and me when my parents were invited out to state dinners and other high-profile events.

We loved Uncle Thabo. He was fun and always gave us his undivided attention.

In 1999 he became president of South Africa.

Funny, I never called him "uncle" when he was president. Never saw him.

The last time I ever spoke to Uncle Thabo was when he babysat me when we lived in Lusaka, Zambia, in the 1970s.

2

There was a strange period when I was in preschool that I would like to include. My dad was asked to lecture on economics at Harvard University in the late 1960s; I was about three years old. We lived in Boston, Massachusetts, in this really neat apartment, compliments of the university. My sister, Sheila, was in Grade One, and I was still in preschool, so most of my time was spent at home with my mother. I remember teaching myself magic tricks while I watched the *Beverly Hillbillies* on American television.

The extraordinary thing about this period in our family's history is that, it being 1968, Dr Martin Luther King and Robert Kennedy were shot during our time in the US. I remember the shock and distress my parents experienced when these events happened. Especially after Dr King's assassination. It felt as if the entire African-American community had gone into mourning, even people who did not necessarily support Dr King's cause. I saw the scene that is played over and over from the archive footage of that time, the one where thousands of people walk with Dr King's coffin—I saw it broadcast live on American television. I remember my mother taking my sister and me to a church that had a memorial service for Dr King in which they played a recording of his famous "I have a dream" speech.

The second year came round pretty quickly, and it soon came time for us to leave. The most vivid image I have of that time is that I was allowed to have my first and last day in Grade One, which began with pledging allegiance to the American flag.

The nature of my father's job meant that as a child I experienced one culture after another.

When I turned fourteen, my parents were called back to Ethiopia from Zambia. This recall coincided with the overthrow of Haile Selassie, the emperor of Ethiopia. The Ethiopian revolution had come to pass. The contrast between the Addis Ababa of my youth, under the rule of the emperor, and Addis Ababa under the rule of the new, young, communist leader Mengistu Haile Miriam was mind-blowing.

As a youngster, living my idyllic life, Ethiopia has fond memories for me. But even at the age of four I remember feeling uncomfortable when the emperor would make his appearances in the streets of Addis Ababa with his huge entourage, followed by a truck with the Lion of Judah in a cage on the back, roaring fiercely at the expectant crowd. Those of us in cars were forced off the road and had to wait for this spectacle to pass before moving on to our various destinations. If you had to be somewhere, tough.

Addis Ababa was a typical African city in that the rich and the poor lived side by side; nothing was hidden. Addis housed a multitude of beggars who would freely roam the streets, urging people to hand over some of their wealth. However, on special state visits Haile Selassie would send the army out to clean up the streets, removing the beggars to goodness knows where. Wherever it was, it couldn't have been far from the city, because when the special state visitor left the beggars were right back on the streets again, ready for business.

When Mengistu took over, we were witness to throngs of working class people walking the streets, heading to various stations that had been set up to educate the people. They were armed with exercise books and pencils and practically marched forward under the harsh gaze of soldiers with AK-47s, who had been ordered to escort them.

The people would file past this huge square in the centre of the city that boasted two gigantic pictures—one of Stalin and one of Lenin. Yes, Addis Ababa had its very own Red Square.

The outsiders looked on with mixed emotions, for on the one hand it was wonderful seeing people who were not able to read and write going to school and being taught how to do so. On the other, we could not help wondering if one form of dictatorship had simply been replaced with another.

While ordinary men and women were being encouraged to get an education, the schools that had existed for the privileged foreigners were being closed down. My parents did not know what to do—at this stage we were approaching our O level years—and in 1976 they reluctantly decided to send my sister, Sheila, and me to boarding school. The only place they felt confident would guarantee us a solid education was the UK, and so we found ourselves on a plane with my mother to England, to Cheltenham.

3

All I really knew of England came from the wonderful holidays we had spent there as a family—all meeting up from different parts of the world. My sister, Quezi, and my brother, Lewis, had by now left home and were living their own lives, carving out their own history, and these reunions in Europe during the European summer were a great reminder that our family had become our country. We knew no other base.

It was heart-wrenching when we finally had to separate from our mother after she delivered us safely to our boarding house. Sheila and I sat looking out of one of the windows of our new home and waved goodbye to her, her tear-stained face a reflection of our own. We watched her till she became a tiny dot in the distance and finally disappeared.

Cheltenham Ladies College. That was where I went to school for the next four years of my life. There we were thrown into the heart of the British establishment. We came from Africa to this school where there were maybe four black students out of nine hundred girls and where the students' parents would pick them up in Bentleys and Rolls-Royces. By the way, an important point. The United Nations paid a large percentage of the school fees of its directors, which is how my parents were able to afford to send us to that school.

We only saw our parents once a year in Ethiopia. For the other two holidays during the course of the year, we caught the train to dear friends of our parents, the Burgesses, who acted as our guardians. Our story is typical of the African experience: parents, because of impossible situations "back home", having to send their children to Europe for a good education. In some cases having to foster their children to people so that they could have a roof over their heads while they studied. This situation is so often misunderstood and is almost always viewed as "abandonment". In truth, it's one of the many consequences of colonisation, that families are forced into making such painful and unnatural decisions, the pressures of which have in so many cases caused those families to splinter.

We spent Christmas and Easter holidays with our guardians in Aberdeen, Scotland. Strangely, during the four years we did this I almost never uttered a word in front of them. I pretty much never spoke. Hard to believe, I know. They were wonderful people. They took good care of us, and while concerned that I didn't speak, they never held it against me.

This was a period of adjustment. England was so different from the Africa we grew up in.

A good example of this was the food.

The Burgesses were great cooks and their meals were always delicious. I mean, the food wasn't awful at school, it couldn't be for the kinds of fees they charged, but it was unbearably plain. Admittedly, we had come from Ethiopia, where the food is as colourful in flavour as it is in appearance. The Burgesses, though, were amazing chefs and they made up for it. The only problem was that their helpings were "English" helpings. Thin slices of meat, one spoon of rice or potatoes, one spoon of veg and so on. I was a teenage African girl with an African appetite. I was starving after every meal! Sheila and I would go shopping in the afternoon and buy loads of junk just to keep us going. Then one day I told Sheila I wasn't going to put up with it anymore. I was going to do an Oliver Twist. I was going to ask for more!

The day I did there was a lot of nervous shuffling and a great deal of apologising, but from then on we got good healthy helpings.

Those dear people—I must have been such a handful. We all know teenagers are impossible at the best of times, never mind when they are somewhat traumatised.

"I was watching television last night and there they were. These black people, they are so destructive that even the devil has abandoned them," said the priest.

Yes, the priest!

Church was not a place I frequented; a hangover from my childhood. My mother was very religious and spiritual. My father was very spiritual but anti the church. The reason for this was that when my grandfather, who was a priest, died, the church threw my grandmother and her children out of the rectory. My father, at twenty-five, became the head of the family and supported them by taking up my grandfather's mantle as a preacher. I often think how extraordinary this must have been for my father. His mouth must have filled with bile every time he had to speak of the things promised in the Bible concerning "the house of God", knowing they had thrown his mother into the street after his father had dedicated his whole life to the church's mission. I often wonder if he took on this role not just to bring in some income but also to try to work out any feelings of revenge he may have carried. My father's focus was always on the "bigger" picture.

I had been dozing off as usual during the mandatory Sunday service when I heard these foul words coming from the man in the pulpit. I froze, not able to comprehend what I was hearing. Just to make sure I wasn't being oversensitive, I looked at my white peers, and when I saw their eyes open wide with horror and embarrassment, I turned to the other black girl in my year and signalled for her to leave that church with me.

This left me branded as a troublemaker for the rest of my time at Cheltenham Ladies College. When I became friendly with a wonderful girl from Sierra Leone, they constantly tried to separate us. One day, the headmistress called me into her office and said: "You and Dawn are beginning to form some kind of ghetto!"

I remember saying to her: "Oh, I see. Where there is more than one black person, we form a ghetto."

Absurd really, but that's what it was. Absurd.

I remember writing a long letter full of anger and despair to my parents. My father responded by telling me not to get distracted. He told me that I was always going to come across small-minded attitudes, that I needed to focus on why I was there, which was, essentially, to get an education so that I could make a difference in the world. He told me to focus on my goals and not to be swayed by these "little interruptions", as he called them.

He was right. I often think of how extraordinary my parents were considering the very difficult life they led as exiles. They made the best of that experience, at the same time working tirelessly to make sure we inherited their values.

"The world owes you nothing," was my father's motto.

I buckled down and left Cheltenham Ladies College with a burning desire to pursue an acting career. My drama teacher in Cheltenham gave me endless encouragement. She even advised me not to feel under any pressure to apply to the mainstream drama schools like RADA (The Royal Academy of Dramatic Arts). Her feeling was that I should focus on learning the craft as opposed to competing for a high-profile career. I am most grateful to this woman, more than she will ever know, because what I have striven for in my career, as a result of my training, is to keep the integrity of the parts I end up playing. Not an easy feat given the shallow mentality that often plagues the visual arts.

When I was accepted by the Welsh College of Music and Drama for a three-year diploma in acting, I wrote to John Matshikiza. Yes, son of Todd Matshikiza, the creator of the legendary musical *King Kong*.

In Zambia, we had been very close to the Mtshikizas. As far as I was concerned, John was one of my big brothers and his mother, Esme, was one of my dearest aunts. They were family. John's untimely death in 2008 still leaves me cold, but I know that, wherever he is, he is still doing great things for his people. I have to say that South Africa treated him very badly. He died of a heart attack brought on by a broken heart in my opinion.

The new South Africa was inevitably partly shaped by the fallout from apartheid. The South African exiles and the children of exiles, because of our insider-outsider status, had learned how to adapt and adjust to all kinds of situations. As a result, many of us have a great deal of confidence. We have had to fight for a place in the societies we were forced to become part of. Inside, there is often a constant battle not to drown under the threat of low self-esteem, but growing up you had no choice but to learn to speak decisively, to look people in the eye and to stand your ground.

Landing in a "free" South Africa was soul-destroying. You were finally part of the majority, but the majority was functioning as a minority. The result—the fighting spirit of the insider-outsider rose to the surface, all that anger that you'd had to keep in check because you were the minority erupted, and because of your confidence, you couldn't hide your frustration when those around you told you that things in South Africa were "different". That you were, in fact, a foreigner. That you had no more rights in South Africa than you'd had where you'd come from. That just because you had been given the vote did not give you the right to use your skills to help build a country. *Your* country.

You were just seen as coming to get what you were entitled to. The more you wanted to share your knowledge, the more you were seen as coming to steal. One was often given honorary white status as long as one stayed in the background. Meanwhile, you were trying to function as the majority and not about to be sidelined. The result was that people were living in a whirlpool of suspicion, jealousy and hatred.

That's when the walls came up and the doors banged shut. Suddenly you realise that you face most days in a haze of alcohol, somehow believing that it might cushion the blows. It doesn't, of course. What it does is subdue your spirit, take all the "fight" out of you till one day you just lie down and die. If not physically then spiritually. It happened to my uncle, who would have been one of the world's great musicians. Eric Nomvete played with the likes of Dollar Brand and now he is dead, and the only memories of him are not his music but his alcoholism. And it happened to me.

What quickly became clear to me was that the one thing that had survived this "positive change" were the well-constructed rules of apartheid, and when you started to challenge those rules, the guillotine came crashing down. Fantastically, it still held South Africa under its spell. John Matshikiza, an example of one of the great Africans who were part of the tapestry of my childhood, was murdered by the apartheid hangover.

As a result of me writing to him, in my last year of drama college, John contacted me and offered me a job with a company called the Bristol Express Theatre Company. He had written a play called *Prophets in the Black Sky,* which was in fact written for two men. However, the company hired two women at John's behest, Cleo Faqu and Pamela Nomvete.

That job launched me into a very successful British stage career that spanned a decade.

Thank you, John.

I understand John revived *Prophets in the Black Sky* in South Africa and had two men playing the parts, as originally intended. What a wonderful dream to come true for him.

In 1994, when I decided to go to South Africa, I had just landed a role at the Royal National Theatre in the UK. I was one of the few blacks who regularly made my way through those prestigious doors at that time. A miracle, really, because nobody ever knew what to do with me. They still don't.

I wasn't black enough, didn't grow up in the ghetto, and I was a strange African—too sure of myself, too comfortable in my own skin.

I was tired. I needed to go to Africa and vote.

SOUTH AFRICA AND ME

1

In April 1994, I landed at Johannesburg International Airport. My state of mind can only be described as euphoric. I hadn't been on African soil for at least fifteen years. My intention was to vote, see my parents vote and discover the country for myself. I decided I would give it two years.

With this "pilgrimage" in mind, I told my parents I would not stay in Cape Town with them. Yes, my parents had returned in 1992.

I explained that if I was going to learn about South Africa, I needed to do it without the comfort and security they had always provided. I had to get to know South Africa on my own terms.

When I was ten, I remember wanting to know about the trials and tribulations my parents had gone through under the apartheid regime, and my father's response to my prodding was always this: "I am not going to tell you because I do not want you to grow up hating a country you know nothing about. One day you will be old enough to go there and discover that land on your own terms."

Well, that time had come.

I got myself an agent and began teaching drama at the Windybrow Theatre. This was the only establishment at the time that encouraged the development of black South African talent. It was here that I bumped into John Matshikiza again, who had also returned to South Africa. He was casting *Julius Caesar* at the Windybrow and, low and behold, John gave me my first job in South Africa. Thus began my artistic and social baptism.

I found myself a flat in Hillbrow, around the corner from the theatre. Yes, Hillbrow!

A young man I was working with, called Themba Ndaba, who is now a well-known actor, director and writer, was so concerned about my safety that he implored me to move into his spare room in the flat he shared with his Canadian wife. I refused. I was brash, showing off. I was from London. I needed to know Johannesburg. Such was my conceit.

I remember those days well because I was earning next-to-nothing at the theatre. I could barely make the rent, so I often had absolutely no money for food. I got into buying fresh-roasted peanuts on the street. For quite some time, that was my staple diet.

I was also working with the star of the hit show *Generations*. He is now a prolific writer-director. This gentleman was playing Archie Moroka, the heartthrob of the show. And it was he who gave me my first lesson in what was to come.

We went out for a while. By then, I had moved in with Themba and his wife, having come out of my building in Hillbrow one day to find myself face-to-face with a dead body for the first time in my life! After that I swallowed my pride and took Themba's offer.

The heartthrob of *Generations* would be most attentive when he was with me during the week, extremely romantic and charming, but every weekend the brother would disappear. I could never get hold of him. Themba used to watch my frustration and laugh. One day, he said: "Welcome to South Africa. This fellow is a township boy. During the week, he is with his girlfriend in town. At the weekend, he is with his girlfriend in the township. You understand?"

I have no idea if that was the case, but I was grateful for Themba's teasing because it prompted me to go to the township. During the week I would, from time to time, go and spend a couple of nights with the heartthrob in Soweto.

I used to love that.

It was the most peaceful experience I had during those early years in Johannesburg. It was wonderful waking up in that simple home, hearing the sounds of people in the houses around, very close. Sometimes, I would even hear a cock crow. It was beautiful.

We would venture out, taking a stroll down the dusty roads that were alive with the citizens of Soweto. These were the people who had captivated the eyes of the world with their dynamic energy. I felt privileged to be among them. Inspired. I had no fear. The place carried the scent of legend, even though it was struggling, pushing through its pain as it was being asked to forget. Asked? No, ordered to forget. It heaved with the memories of past heroes. It limped along while trying to make sense of its new status in the new South Africa.

Soweto.

The heartthrob had given me my first glimpse of this land's treasure as I moved among the people of Soweto.

This was a most exciting time in South Africa. I was finding my feet and the country was doing the same. I met lots and lots of people, some of them foreign-born South Africans like myself who I knew from the past. We dialogued, we created, we dreamed, we fought, we made love and we all forged a way ahead in the "new South Africa". Some said it was akin to the Wild West—in a way, how right they were. I told myself that if I could make it in this place, I could make it anywhere.

The heartthrob introduced me to the producers of *Generations*. I auditioned for them and landed the role of Ntsiki Lukhele in this show that portrayed successful black people in the corporate arena. Rich, beautiful and ambitious.

I landed the role of "the bitch". My life changed forever.

I rose in about two years from being a no-name English actress to being one of the biggest household names South Africa had ever seen.

Life as I knew it changed completely.

I bought my first house: a beautiful two-bedroom, two-bathroom townhouse in a place called North Gate. I loved that place. Living room, dining room and separate kitchen. I even had a little garden and a small veranda to boot. What a feeling to own property. My parents were brimming with pride as they watched me rise from bohemian artist to high-earning television success story.

If only life was like the movies.

This would have been the happy ending. Girl finds her way back to her roots and rises from rags to riches. *The End.*

Unfortunately, life just isn't like that.

Ntsiki became ever more popular, to the point where it was even a little uncomfortable living in a complex. Random people started knocking on my door. When I opened it, they would often shove kids in my face, toddlers who couldn't possibly know who I was. They would then try to invite themselves in for tea, to "talk". I would get these proposals in all kinds of dialects and accents. This was the new South Africa, after all. The "rainbow" nation. I stopped opening my door.

This did nothing to stop the intrusion into my sanctuary.

They began to gather on my little patch of garden and watch me through the window as if they were watching television. So I stopped opening my curtains. My world was becoming more and more isolated and dark.

What I didn't realise was that this was happening to me emotionally and spiritually as well. My world was shutting down.

It became harder and harder to walk out of the front door without being accosted. Forming genuine friendships became nearly impossible. I learned how not to trust anyone. My life was slowly becoming consumed by the persona of Ntsiki.

Increasingly, I found pleasure in my own company, the only company I could trust. Only I didn't. Not enough. I was losing perspective.

From time to time, I would visit my parents in Cape Town and wallow in their love and support. I felt such a fake, unable to share their joy at my resounding success.

I was on the cover of every magazine. I was always doing television, radio and press interviews.

Even my poor parents had to contend with the fans when they realised who they were. Fame is such a strange thing. You end up having to protect your loved ones from its relentless, merciless, slashing claws.

You know, I remember years before this, sitting in my flat in London that I shared with Sheila, watching a soap star being interviewed, and thinking: *I want that for my life.*

What comes to mind? How does the saying go? "Be careful what you wish for."

Yep, I had unwittingly planted that seed and now it had taken root.

By now, the heartthrob and I had broken up and I had all kinds of suitors making a bid for my attention. It was kind of scary; I was losing focus and had consequently lost the ability to be discerning. It got to a point where I felt I needed a partner for protection, just to say I was with somebody. To show you how I had lost my way, I ended up having an affair with a producer who I will call Forbidden Lover. He was one of the rising, successful black producers, so in my mind just the right energy to be around. The only problem was that he had a live-in girlfriend, so we could not go public with our relationship. I was all over the place. And it was in the midst of this confusion that I met Farai Sapiens.

I had been performing in a play at the Market Theatre, *The Good Woman of Sharkville*, directed by Janet Suzman, an adaptation of Brecht's *The Good Person of Szechwan*. I met him because he had accompanied a friend of mine to the play. Funny, I never saw that guy again after that night. Don't you find that sometimes? People are brought into your life for a reason, and when they have served that purpose, they simply vanish? This dude delivered Farai to me.

After the show, I met them at Nicky's, this really cool jazz bar across the road from the Market Theatre. High from the performance and feeling totally open, I remember being fascinated by this young man— he was seven years younger than me. He seemed different. Articulate, energetic, insightful and not at all fazed by being in the presence of the biggest "bitch" on television. The woman everyone loved to hate. He didn't refer to it once, which I found incredibly refreshing.

Farai loved to see himself as an experienced hustler, so I guess part of his "hustle" was not to react to who I was so I would feel comfortable and at ease. That night, when I climbed into my Mercedes Benz 180c Class, I had a warm, fuzzy feeling inside. I never imagined I would see Farai again, but I was glad I had spent the evening with him.

If only it had ended there.

Several weeks later, there was a party at the production offices I now owned with my Forbidden Lover and Themba Ndaba. We decided to celebrate the completion of the first project we had co-produced. It was called *Flat 27*. Themba and I had co-written this comedy that we felt gave a glimpse into the complex characters that made up the new South Africa.

We invited my dad to the party, as he was in Johannesburg on business. So all in all, it was a great night and we all felt this amazing sense of achievement.

My Forbidden Lover thought my dad was viewing him as a future son-in-law. Makes me giggle now when I think of it, because he couldn't have been further from the truth.

After the party, we business partners decided to go dancing at a club in Rosebank. The club was heaving that night, completely in keeping with our mood—we were feeling totally and utterly invincible. We were the new South Africa, the happening new black elite. You can smell it, can't you?

At the club, lo and behold, suddenly out of the bodies bouncing up and down to the beat, Farai Sapiens morphed into view. I smiled with glee, remembering this refreshing young man's name. Consumed by the moment, I danced suggestively with Farai and gave him my number, much to the irritation of Forbidden Lover. His discomfort was something from which I derived a great deal of pleasure.

I was very drunk and feeling extremely reckless, having consumed a fair amount of Champagne. Forbidden Lover at some point in the evening whispered in my ear that he and his girlfriend had split up and that she had moved out. He then suggested that I follow him home. All I can say is that my libido took over. It was all so dangerous, so out of control. I was falling further and further down a very dark and slippery slope.

We sped along the motorway to his house. I could barely focus. I was so drunk, I didn't see the police van that seemed to come out of nowhere. The whole front of my Mercedes was damaged badly, and my car had to be towed away. To be honest I don't know why I didn't land in jail. Maybe Forbidden Lover greased the palm of the police officers. I don't know. My life had come to a crashing halt, but instead of stopping and taking heed of this humongous warning, I shoved it aside, climbed into Forbidden Lover's car and landed in his bed for the night.

In the morning, I woke up to this woman staring down at me and telling me to get out of her bed.

Forbidden Lover and I froze. The woman in question, his so-called "ex" live-in lover, was clearly back. I was stuck under the covers, watching this weird, vicious shouting match happening over my head. I couldn't move—I was completely naked under those sheets!

He finally steered her out of the room and I ran into the bathroom to put on my clothes. I remember sliding to the floor in complete shame. I felt like a whore. I was a whore in more ways than one. I had created a very, very bad cause for my life. I was feeding a beast in my psyche I had never met before, and all it wanted was fame and money.

2

Morning sickness is the worst thing ever when you don't want what it signifies. I was pregnant, and the baby could only belong to the one man I was sleeping with. My Forbidden Lover. Stupidly, just before that fateful night when I had smashed my car into a police van, he and I, in a fit of passion, had had unprotected sex in the back of his car.

So, during that splurge of events when I had wrecked my car, given Farai my phone number and been caught in a bed I shouldn't have been in, I had also been carrying this secret that finally was revealed: I was pregnant.

I went off Forbidden Lover immediately. I was actually repulsed by him, but I decided to have the baby. At twenty-three I had aborted a child because I was still in college and couldn't face parenting. Now in my thirties, I wasn't about to prevent another child from entering the world.

I arranged an audience with the father because I felt he had a right to know, but I also wanted to tell him I didn't expect anything from him. I would do this on my own. I then told my parents, who supported me all the way. Those people were amazing. I miss them both. I am glad to say they both passed in the land of their birth. They may not have been allowed to live here for over fifty years, but at least they are buried here.

Having to be around the father of my unborn child—we shared a production office—was pretty strenuous. The tension between us was palpable and our mutual disgust for each other was something neither of us could hide.

The daily phone calls from young Farai were therefore like manna from heaven.

I felt unclean and talking to him was like standing under a long shower for a couple of hours, washing my sins away. Perhaps my real reason for keeping the baby was as a form of punishment for my dishonourable behaviour. Farai made me feel that I was worth something.

I found myself meeting up with Farai frequently. His company was always so refreshing and he made it all seem so innocent.

I learned about his somewhat traumatic upbringing. He was the eldest of four boys and had two stepsisters. His mother had been the victim of relentless physical abuse at the hands of his father. There had been a time when they were affluent, his father had been a successful businessman, but for some reason he had lost everything and ended up living in a township-like dwelling with his second wife and two children. It happens. One day you have everything, the next day you are left with nothing. Those are the times you are forced to stop, take stock of what you have surrounded yourself with and decide on which path you will take next.

It's an opportunity to see how one has chosen to define oneself.

One of Farai's younger brothers had been diagnosed as HIV positive and his mother could barely string two cents together. They all wanted the life they'd once had back. They absolutely refused to accept what had happened. Interestingly, his father, who I met later on in our relationship, was the only one of them that had accepted it and had totally surrendered. He'd given up. With the declining economic climate in Zimbabwe, I guess he was the realist.

For the rest of the family, they took on the character of marauding wolves, which is exactly what a hungry stomach and lack of self-belief can do to one.

I had a break coming up and decided to go to the UK. My parents had gone on holiday and I felt I wanted to be close to them, even though they were in Cambridge and I was going to be with my sister in London. I just needed to get away. Be anonymous for a bit. Get some perspective. Little did I know I was about to send myself even deeper into the black hole that was rapidly becoming my reality.

The night before I left for London, Farai visited. When it came time for him to leave, he grabbed me unceremoniously and planted a long, wet kiss on my lips. I vaguely responded. A little shocked and maybe flattered? One thing that struck me, though, is that I was devoid of passion. Come to think of it, I didn't feel any coming from him either.

Two people lost. Two people who had absolutely no idea who they were and what it was they wanted to contribute to the world—really frightening, really disturbing and really, really dangerous.

It was wonderful to be back in London, the "first world", where everything "worked". I was anonymous again: a faceless, nameless being, just a number, a statistic. Not Ntsiki, the "bitch" from *Generations*; I didn't have to worry about being stared at or signing the hundredth autograph of the day.

I could catch the efficient, impersonal Tube that would take me from A to B. I didn't have to sit in a car and travel long, exhausting distances, shooing away the guy who enthusiastically tried to clean my windscreen for a few extra bucks.

I could just sit and stare ahead of me into nothingness and slowly fade from view. Here in London I could be invisible and I welcomed it.

My sister, Sheila, was thrilled I was pregnant and immediately declared that this was our baby. Suddenly being pregnant was beginning to feel wonderful.

I remember that night when *it* happened like it was yesterday. I remember sitting in the restaurant in Clapham Common with one of my oldest and dearest friends, Richard Santhiri, having just named him as godfather to my child. I remember going to the bathroom and seeing the first drops of blood.

I remember stumbling out of that cubicle, flashes of a dream I'd had when I first discovered I was pregnant filling my mind. I was having a shower and blood began to pour out of me, and all I kept saying was: "Oh, my God, I've lost it!"

Was this happening for real now?

I was back in the main part of the restaurant and asking for the phone. I wanted to talk to my mother. My mother . . .

The woman who nurtured me, the woman who created a country for her family out of love since there was no physical place we could run back to.

My mother has now passed on. Every bone in my body appreciates every action she ever took to keep our sense of identity intact. Even after she'd had a nervous breakdown and it felt like some of her dynamism had gone, even then she protected all of us with the ferocity of a lioness.

So, naturally, it was my mother who I called when I saw that spot of blood in the restroom of the restaurant in Clapham.

My mother had trained and worked as a nurse before she became the wife of a United Nations economist. Her advice was that I go home right away and monitor the bleeding. She told me that if it continued or got heavier, then I should get to a hospital immediately. The future godfather to my child paid the bill and put me safely into a taxi bound for my sister's flat.

When I got there, Sheila wrapped me up in a blanket and I lay down on the couch in the living room. We talked and laughed, creating positive future memories for the child that was hanging on so precariously to life.

On my next visit to the bathroom I was met with more blood, a little heavier this time.

We found ourselves in the casualty wing of the Royal Free Hospital in North London at midnight.

It was surreal as we waited patiently to be seen by a doctor. We tried to joke and talk about better days, struggling to come to terms with what was really happening.

Finally, we were called. A tall female doctor with blonde hair and a very warm but efficient manner led us into the consulting rooms. Nervously, I explained to her what had happened. I remember her professional gaze changing to a look of unreserved compassion. She asked me to get onto the bed so she could check for the heartbeat of the child. The gel went onto my belly and the ultrasound machine was switched on.

The doctor searched and searched for the heartbeat as we all held our breath. Finally, she said she detected a faint movement that was baby's heart.

She suggested we go home and monitor the bleeding. Looking back, I think she wanted to believe as much as we did that the baby was going to make it.

Sheila and I went home. We sat up all night, willing our little friend to live. At about three am I went to the bathroom to check for the last time. It was definitely flowing more freely now. We were in the car once again that morning, on the way to the hospital.

This time the wait was very short. I found myself looking into the kindest eyes—they belonged to a tall doctor from India. He gently explained that a nurse would come and check the heartbeat on the ultrasound. On that bed again, Sheila standing next to me, palms pressed together in silent prayer. I stared at the screen as the image of the foetus came into view. Actually, my memory is of a fully formed baby. That's what I saw, which is impossible as the foetus was only three months old. The nurse searched for the heartbeat, but this time we all could see nothing was happening. She shook her head and announced she couldn't find it. I remember looking up at her and saying: "So, it's dead?"

With great difficulty, she nodded. "There's no heartbeat," she said.

Sheila burst into tears while I stared at what looked to me like a perfectly formed baby.

Eventually the nurse turned off the machine and the doctor took over. With great compassion he explained that because the baby had not completely aborted itself they would have to carry out a procedure to remove the foetus from my womb to avoid me being poisoned.

The doctor who would birth my dead baby was a wonderful, young Irish woman with soft red curls. I believed in angels then, and I believed, for a long time, that she and the Indian doctor were angels come to support me as they carried my baby safely across to the afterlife. I still believe that they were specially chosen to do just that. They were great human spirits.

The Irish doctor explained that women often miscarry in the first trimester. She said that I must not blame myself. She told me that there was nothing I could have done to save the baby's life. She was wrong. I could have not had an affair with a man who belonged to someone else. I could have waited for my prince to come and decided to have a child out of love. I could have done the right thing.

I had two weeks left of my holiday. I spent it with my parents in Cambridge. I remember clearly the day I called the father of the child and told him that I had lost it. He was silent for quite some time and then simply thanked me for letting him know. Sometime after all this, he confessed that he believed I had gone to England to terminate the pregnancy. Such arrogance. Brother hadn't believed me when I'd told him that I didn't want him to be a part of our lives.

"Deep," as the Americans would say.

SLAVE AT HOME, SLAVE AT WORK

1

I returned to South Africa and was immediately in "Ntsiki" mode. No privacy, lots of exposure and Farai Sapiens was now becoming entrenched in my life.

It all started to take root when we kind of carried on where we had left off. The first time I called, we arranged to meet at my house, my sanctuary, which had now become the isolation ward from which I sustained the fantasy world that I had lost control of at the birth of Ntsiki.

I remember having this long heart-to-heart with Farai, where I set a timeline for any kind of physical relationship we may embark on. I was feeling fragile. I had just miscarried. He listened patiently and was extremely respectful of my needs.

Our friendship developed and he slowly started to introduce me to members of his family. The one character I will never forget and on who, I am sure, I will base a number of characters, was Farai's brother, the one I will call the Artful Dodger.

The Artful Dodger was soft-spoken and very, very intelligent. It was never clear what he did for a living. It seemed to be a bit of this and a bit of that. From time to time, I would overhear strange, incomprehensible conversations between Farai and the Artful Dodger concerning joint "business ventures". In my naiveté I never asked what these joint ventures might be. Or maybe it wasn't naiveté, maybe it was fear. But fear of what? Fear that I may well have to wake up to the fact that in the space I was in, at this time, genuine friendships were not forthcoming?

The Artful Dodger was always respectful towards me, but I knew that when he looked at me he saw Ntsiki—he even said as much. To a man like the Artful Dodger, this meant money, perhaps even fame, but certainly a platform from which he could further his "business".

When your self-esteem has reached rock bottom, when you are in hell, you will attract others in this dark place, and, of course, the predators start to close in.

I remember waking up one morning, after the Artful Dodger had spent the night, to a big, blank space where my television and DVD player had been. By now, Farai had semi moved in and his brother would often spend the night. My space, that had once been just for me, had been overrun. The outside world had graduated from *wanting* to come in to actually *moving* in. I had opened the door, I had opened the curtains, but instead of letting the sun in, I had opened myself up to greed born of desperation.

Farai didn't even fight me when I accused his brother. He kind of shrugged his shoulders and made a face that said: "Well, that's my brother for you."

It didn't take long for me to figure out that the Artful Dodger was a professional thief.

As time went on and I met more of Farai's Zimbabwean brethren, they always looked at me in horror at the mention of the Artful Dodger. They literally shivered.

I had the misfortune of meeting one of the mothers of one of the Artful Dodger's children. She had nothing pleasant to say about the Artful Dodger. I remember that one day she decided to be candid with me. She told me that the Artful Dodger was not only a thief but also a bona fide criminal. She told me how he had robbed banks and laundered money in her house. She told me how he had come home to her on several occasions with money that had blood on it. She told me how he had physically abused her—the two of them used to have fistfights.

One day, having returned from speaking to her, I told Farai I never wanted to see his brother again. Ever. If he set foot in our house ever again I would call the police. However, I did not do this immediately after I learned of the psychotic behaviour of his brother; I did this about a year later.

Where had I gone? Where was my reason? Where had I placed my boundaries?

I was nowhere. I had no boundaries. It was as if I were dead or dying.

Not long after this, Farai announced that his mother was coming to South Africa to buy groceries. I had explained to Farai that for me space was an absolute must and assumed his mother had a place to stay since she had come to Johannesburg for the purpose of buying goods for quite some time. I was looked upon as mean and lacking in African hospitality. His mother would be where her son was, even though he didn't officially live with me.

He worked, but he wasn't paying any bills, buying food or contributing to the bond.

In my confusion, not wanting to appear cruel or mean and needing to come across as caring and considerate, needing to be identified as a different person from the insensitive, cold, ambitious, ruthless Ntsiki, I had unwittingly woven a web of self-delusion and placed myself firmly in a hell of powerlessness.

Having Farai's mother in the house was an experience that is hard to explain. I will refer to this lady as the Puppeteer.

I went from cooking meals that were a result of my global identity to cooking only Zimbabwean cuisine because Farai's mother had a sensitive stomach and was not used to the variety of spices I liked to experiment with. As a result, I began to dislike being in the kitchen. Suddenly, cooking became a duty, not an exercise in creative expression.

The Puppeteer would often intimate to me that a "good African wife" cooked what satisfied her husband, gave him what he wanted in bed and kept quiet if he frequently came home drunk and reeking of another woman's perfume. I remember her adding snidely that I could be forgiven for not understanding, being from England, but I would learn. Now that I think of it, the woman was warning me of things to come, or rather she was *grooming* me for things to come, but I was just too obtuse to comprehend that.

I used to have a lady, a wonderful woman, who cleaned my house twice a week. Unfortunately, she died after being run over by a car on her way to work one day. It was devastating to learn of something so horrific, but I came to realise very early on that these kinds of scenarios were regular occurrences in the harsh landscape that is Johannesburg.

That wonderful woman cleaned my house as if it had been her own. Now that my house was filling up, I employed another lady to help me clean every day. What had happened to my space, my sanctuary? Where was I supposed to breathe, to touch base with myself? At work I was dealing with the constant challenge of not having an outlet for my own creative expression. At home I did not have the space to undress either physically or mentally. I was on twenty-four-hour alert. I couldn't step out of my house without being recognised by people needing me to acknowledged them. I couldn't return home and be myself. The spaces were shrinking, my exit points were blocked. I had forgotten how to live. I couldn't see. My arteries felt like they were clogging up. And all the time, the Sapienses were settling deeper and deeper into my sanctuary, taking every piece of my peace as they did so.

The horror of it was that I was giving them permission to do it.

Zimbabwe had lost sight of itself. Power and greed had sunk their ugly teeth into it, and now the people of Zimbabwe had been stripped of all sense of worth. The will to survive was the only driving force, and those in their path, woe betide them.

Late one night, the Puppeteer arrived on my doorstep for one of her three monthly visits to buy groceries to take back "home". When we opened the door, the frail figure accompanying her practically fell into the house.

Farai announced the new arrival as yet another one of his brothers. This woman had given her husband so many sons, so many heirs, and yet still she wasn't with him. What this must have done to her, I cannot imagine.

In many African traditions, to bear a man sons bestows upon you the greatest respect. She had been left with nothing and was consequently now training her sons to become expert thieves.

This young man was very, very ill. He had full-blown AIDS. When he came to the house, he could hardly stand. His eyes were rolled back into his head and he was incoherent.

His arrival meant an extra mouth to feed and—after we finally got him to a doctor (he was in complete denial about his condition)—medical bills that were astronomical. As soon as he was diagnosed so began the whole horrific antiviral routine. This was an ongoing exercise, and I was paying for it as none of the Sapienses was earning. By now Farai had left his corporate job and was looking for something else. His efforts were somewhat erratic and half-hearted. He didn't seem to know what he was good at or what he wanted to do. One of his brief escapades involved running a nightclub. The two gentlemen who owned the club needed someone with a marketing background to help them build their business. How Farai found out about this opportunity I will never know, but he did.

To be honest, this is where I felt Farai belonged. He was good at managing the club. His two bosses/potential future partners were really good to him, and for a while the whole thing worked. But if Farai had one problem it was that he could never stick to anything and see it through. If he wasn't realising a million straight away, he would decide that whatever it was wasn't for him. He talked a good game, but he wasn't too good at sticking to a plan. And it didn't help that he was in the spotlight—in a relationship with the biggest bitch on television.

My success was a dream come true for Farai and his biggest nightmare.

A dream because he could spend money on looking and smelling good, he was invited to fancy gatherings, he drove a fancy car and was photographed all the time. He could pretend he was a Hollywood star along with the rest of the folk in the burgeoning South African film and television industry.

A nightmare because none of it was his doing, so the attention was never on him for what he had achieved. This drove him crazy. He wanted me out of the way, but he needed me.

The house was shrinking with all the bodies crowding into it. We needed a bigger place, and we got it. A beautiful house in an affluent neighbourhood called Randpark Ridge. The house had two storeys. It had a large kitchen, a dining room, a living room, a study, a TV room and four bedrooms—the main bedroom even had its own en suite bathroom. Now I was really living like a famous person. Now I could keep the outside world at bay.

I rented out my first house for a year, then I sold it—the demands on my finances made keeping it impossible.

2

At this point I was unable to work on any other projects. *Generations* and Ntsiki had now become my life. She was huge, like JR in Dallas in the 1980s. I was constantly trying to explain that Ntsiki was the character I was playing and bore no resemblance to Pamela, but no one was listening. The more I tried to speak up, the more I felt beaten down. The weapon that was consistently used against me was that I was a foreigner and therefore had no right to an opinion. This was communicated ever so subtly, but it was extraordinarily effective—with my ranting falling on deaf ears I began to implode. The poison was seeping into my system; I was becoming toxic to myself.

There was a most interesting set-up at *Generations* where the producers of the show would host several social gatherings a week for the cast and crew. These took the form of wild parties with copious amounts of alcohol floating freely around. On the whole these gatherings had a hundred per cent turnout, every time, because people just wanted to drown their sorrows—they wanted to anesthetise themselves against the insane, unbalanced lives we were living.

The discrepancies we experienced while working on a successful show in the SABC, in the new South Africa, were many. For example, one morning one of the make-up women suddenly burst into tears while working on my face. I asked her what the matter was. She explained to me that she lived in a two-room house in Soweto and that she desperately wanted to build an extension so that her teenage son could have his own room and not have to continue sleeping on the floor in her and her husband's bedroom. The only problem was she couldn't afford the R1 000 it would cost to build it. I suggested she simply ask for a loan from the producers—with it being such a small amount of money, I was sure they would agree to some kind of modest repayment plan since she was a permanent employee. This was the most successful show in the country and I was certain they would take care of their workers. Later that day I caught up with her to find out if she'd managed to solve her problem. She told me she had asked for the loan and had been turned down. I couldn't believe it. What was worse is that this was one of the senior make-up artists on the most successful television show in the country, and her wage couldn't cover her building a small extension to her already ridiculously tiny dwelling.

The discrepancies didn't stop there. Some of the performers, even though they were on the covers of magazines and did appearances at high-profile events, were still living in one-bedroomed dwellings in the township. Many had responsibilities, being the sole breadwinners in their families. In most cases, these were young people in their twenties.

The pressure these young, talented people were under was overwhelming.

I should have been there for them. My circumstances were nowhere near as gruelling as theirs. Instead, I was trying to make sense of my own life while working in this distorted and grotesque arena. I would go to these wild soirees and drive home plastered, usually very, very late. It started with Friday nights and then accelerated to three or four times a week.

Farai began to complain. We started to bicker constantly about my habit of staying out with the cast and crew till late, then driving home drunk. This looks like concern on the surface, but I soon learned it was because he wasn't in control of the situation. This was a world he wanted in on but was permanently stuck on the edge of.

All the warnings, I realise now, were there, every step of the way on my journey to fame. If I had given myself a moment to reflect, I would have seen that nothing was clear; my life was out of focus and chaotic. I was surrounded by, and was myself the living example of, pure insanity.

One night, after returning home in a haze as usual and grateful to be alive, I walked into the house and found Farai sitting on our bed. He looked off centre. The mirror on my dressing table had been smashed and there were glass fragments lying everywhere. I then looked down at his hand and he was bleeding. I remember a cold feeling encircling my heart, and without saying a word I went to the spare room for the night. Needless to say, his little performance worked, because I stopped going to the *Generations* parties.

My world continued to have no direction. I had nothing to lean on, just an infinite black hole, and I was falling, falling, falling. The world around me continued to reflect the chaos within.

I remember one particular scenario that to this day has me reeling. A wonderfully talented actress, who obviously had some serious psychological problems—highlighted by the fact that she lived in her dressing room—was dismissed as being a "problem". The attitude was that she needed to pull herself together. When I first found out that this woman was living in her dressing room, I went to the producers and asked them if they knew this was going on. They laughed it off and said that I would soon learn all about this girl, that she was trouble and they weren't interested in entertaining her antics.

I suggested they perhaps send her for therapy, as she was in a sense under their care since she was one of their stars. I remember their eyes glazing over as they promised to look into it.

This woman's condition deteriorated on a daily basis and it soon got to the point where she was unable to come on set sober. To be honest, this was not an unusual state of affairs. There were days I would come to work and they would have to cancel the shoot because actors had turned up to work completely incoherent. Even though I was consuming copious amounts of alcohol daily, my professionalism refused to allow me to drink during working hours, so I found this state of affairs pretty disgusting. I complained constantly about it, to the point where my attitude began to make me unpopular with not only the producers but also my fellow actors. They felt I had placed myself on a pedestal, coming from the British stage and all. They were right. A great deal of snobbery was seeping through because my thoughts were that this would never have been allowed to happen in England. I did feel that the management was basically incompetent. *How dare I?* You are probably thinking. Yes, how dare I? This is where England had done a great job. Here we were, we children of exiles, adopting some of the superiority born of being products of the British system.

In many ways we felt we knew better and there were some elements in this "African" way of doing things that needed changing.

Instead of really trying to understand and help with finding solutions, this attitude drove me to take action that meant I caused more damage than good.

My relentless complaining meant that, to shut me up, they targeted the most vulnerable person in the whole debacle.

The unstable actress took to coming on set wearing a huge winter coat which, when discarded, revealed her naked body. It got to the point where she would roam the corridors of the SABC dressed only in that coat. My complaints, my allegations of incompetence and lack of respect for artists led to this girl being fired from the show. It came as a terrible shock to everyone—she was one of the most popular characters!

Now that I think of it, this was a warning just to show us who was boss.

Meanwhile, my home, the place I should have been able to come back to and recuperate in, was filling up with Farai's relatives. There was now his ailing brother, the Puppeteer and another younger brother of Farai's who because of the situation in Zimbabwe could not find work. The hope was that he would find some and then try to get into college in South Africa. I will call him Artful Dodger Jr. He hung around the house for over a year doing absolutely nothing. Eventually it was revealed that he had hooked up with the Artful Dodger and had embarked on a life of crime.

Let me describe one horrendous day for you and demonstrate what my life looked like.

One morning, I got up early, as usual, and dashed out of the house before any of the Sapienses woke up, so that I wouldn't have to deal with their demands. These included Farai's ailing brother wanting me to go and pick up a prescription for him, the Puppeteer wanting me to give her money so that she could buy a house for herself "back home" in Zimbabwe and Farai wanting the car because he had some "business meetings".

On arrival at the SABC, having changed into my Ntsiki costume for the day, I made my way to the make-up room. The make-up artists looked strained. They informed me that one of the actresses had turned up drunk and the day was made up mostly of her scenes. It was so bad that the producers had told her to sleep it off—they would see what she was like in the next couple of hours. Consequently, the rest of us just had to wait. Furious; I stomped off to the studios to see if I could catch one of the producers. Instead, I bumped, unceremoniously, into the actress who was playing opposite the drunk that day. This woman was swaying and reeked of alcohol. When I asked her what the hell was going on, she responded: "If you can't beat them, join them."

I promptly left for my dressing room, changed and waited for word that I could go home. It came four and a half hours later. As I walked towards the exit, lying on the floor of one of the corridors was the actress I had bumped into earlier. Her dress was halfway up her waist and she was singing out of tune. I tried to get her up but it was useless. She was too far gone. This woman was in her early fifties. I left her there.

What had become of me? I left her there.

I went straight to the nearest bar and downed two or three shots, in preparation for what awaited me at home.

When I walked through the door, a middle-aged gentleman was sitting in the lounge, a small suitcase at his feet. I was to discover that this surprise guest was an uncle of Farai's who had come to stay for a few days. Yet another houseguest! *Permanent or semi-permanent,* I wondered.

That night, Farai and I had a celebrity dinner to go to.

We got back home at about two in the morning. It was a Friday, I remember. As we pulled up to the garage. I saw a young girl sitting on the ground, waiting patiently. Puzzled, I got out of the car and asked if I could help her. She responded by telling me that she had come all the way from Bloemfontein. She had somehow found out where Ntsiki lived, because she knew that she was the only person who could help her. This child claimed she came from an abusive home and did not want to go back.

We took her into the house, gave her some food and, as soon as she had eaten, promptly took her to the police station. There the police interrogated the girl and it transpired that she had an aunt in Bloemfontein. The police got the aunt's details and suggested we inform her of her niece's whereabouts.

They called a few shelters and found one that would take her.

The police warned us not to let the girl stay in our house, as there had apparently been many such cases which had ended with the girl accusing the man of the house of rape. This then led to extortion by the "victim", another cruel money-making scheme.

We started the long drive to the shelter that had a vacancy—it was called Angels and was a forty-five minute drive from the station. After about half an hour, we began to leave behind buildings and lights and seemed to enter dense farmland. At some point, we turned off the tarmac and found ourselves on a bumpy dirt road. I turned to check on our passenger. Up to this point, her expression had been bland, uninterested. Even when she had relayed her fairly disturbing reasons for travelling to Johannesburg, there had been little or no expression. Now the blank mask had been replaced with a decided look of panic.

Finally, a ghostly sign materialised out of the dark with *Angels* painted on it. Dogs started leaping at the car windows and, as the car headlights swept the yard, a group of people stumbled out of what looked like a series of rundown buildings. An overweight, blonde woman in a dirty nightdress, holding a baby, came towards the car. I got out to greet her and noticed a brood of dirty, snot-nosed children from all ethnic backgrounds following her. Suddenly, from somewhere out of the dark, three or more strange-looking men, smoking, loomed into view.

I exchanged a few niceties with this woman who could barely speak English as more children, now a little older, came spilling out of what I can only describe as a hovel. The woman confirmed she was expecting the girl we had in the car.

I went round and opened the door to let her out. She froze. A tear rolled down her cheek. I urged her to get out of the car. Eventually she did.

With the girl safely delivered to the Angels, I got back into the car and we set off home through the pitch-black African night.

Chugging along, Farai just kept saying that we couldn't leave the girl there. My heart sank because I felt the same way, but I was also burning with resentment. The house was full of his relatives and now I was expected to take in strays from the street. I was a famous South African soap opera actress, not Rockefeller.

Rockefeller or not, we couldn't leave that girl there. In no time, Farai had turned the car around and we were headed back to Angels. When we found the young girl, she practically ran to the car. The look of relief on her face was indescribable. It was right not to leave her there, but I couldn't get the warnings from the police out of my mind. She was desperate and hungry for a better life. She wanted to live like Ntsiki.

I told her that first thing in the morning I would call her aunt and she was going back to stay with her. The next morning I did just that. Her aunt was beside herself with relief that the child was safe and begged us to send her home. I drove the young girl to the station, bought her a ticket and sent her on her way.

When you are famous in Africa there are no boundaries. You are accessible and people relate to you as the character you are playing— there is no filter. As Ntsiki, I provided hope in a land where black women were basically invisible. The birth of Ntsiki marked a change in the place of black women in South African society. They now had a voice and they wanted to be heard by any means necessary. The only problem was that what was being presented on screen was a totally false representation of what my life actually looked like.

3

It was the moment of a lifetime. *Generations* now had the royal stamp of approval. The main cast and the producers had been invited to meet with President Nelson Mandela. For me, this was better than winning an Oscar. I really didn't care if I ever made it to Hollywood at that moment—the fact that I had been invited to an audience with Madiba meant that I must have done something right!

Being a celebrity in South Africa meant that you were almost always left standing on the sidelines, while stars from America and the UK seemed to have free access to the rulers of our land. Yet in the eyes of the South African people, we were heroes. We were always celebrated and our beloved fans never tired of telling us how much joy we brought them.

If you will allow me, I would like to take a moment to describe the kinds of scenarios South African celebrities often found themselves in.

It was the opening of a historic venue and all us "celebrities" had been invited.

Some people had a problem with us being given the title of celebrity, because, I guess, in their minds you had to have a villa in Spain, be plagued by the paparazzi and be nominated for at least a BAFTA before you could wear the mantle of celebrity. We wore it because the people of South Africa declared it, and that was okay with us.

I had travelled all over the country, making appearances, and everywhere they knew Ntsiki and *Generations* and they loved it—even in the most remote areas. They could name all the main characters, and the minor ones for that matter. Even the street kids managed to find a way to sneak into shop or bar doorways to watch *Generations*.

The special guest at the opening of this historic venue was to be none other than our very own president, Nelson Mandela. We all arrived in style and were led into the foyer, where we were to meet and greet one another.

Also joining us, or so we thought, only to learn that we were seen as actually joining them, were a group of American film stars. This group included Danny Glover and Morgan Freeman.

It all seemed pretty natural and quite wonderful, even though when I was introduced to Danny Glover I felt as if I should bow or something. There was such a furore around him that I forgot for a moment that he was just another actor, like me.

Then it happened. As we looked on, he and the other American stars were led into what was called a VIP area. The South African celebrities followed, naturally, and were promptly and unceremoniously stopped at the door.

We were barked at and told that the area was for VIPs only. We were then herded outside and plonked in front of a huge French window so we could see our American counterparts having an audience with our beloved president. It was almost vindictive of the organisers—it was if they were hell-bent on showing us that we just weren't good enough. Was this perhaps another hangover of separate development? Only this time we weren't separated by ethnicity or class but by international standards of success. It would have been hilarious had it not been so tragic.

You can imagine, then, what a triumph it was when the cast of *Generations* were told that Tata wanted to see us at his residence for lunch. Especially when we learned that this had been his own personal request. Awesome! I will have to boast for a second because when we stood in line to greet him, he did stop in front of me and say: "I am so happy. I am so happy to see you."

I stared stupidly at him, wanting to throw myself prostrate and thank him for making me feel that being recognised for what you do in your homeland can feel just as good as being cast in a production in some foreign land.

Recently, I was performing at the Royal Shakespeare Theatre in Stratford, England—Shakespeare's birthplace. We, the cast, were invited backstage to meet Prince Charles. As with meeting Tata, we stood in line to greet the prince. He acknowledged the home-grown British actors he was familiar with but didn't really engage with the rest of us. He was wonderfully polite, but I meant nothing to him. In contrast, in front of the father of my homeland I felt acknowledged. I felt dizzy; my heart was full.

That was one of the most wonderful afternoons I had ever spent in my life and the memory of it will forever be engraved in my heart.

Unfortunately, once it was over, I had to return home and face the music.

The following morning at about six am, there was a knock on our bedroom door. We groggily responded and were promptly greeted by Farai's uncle's voice, which asked us both to come downstairs.

As we stumbled down the stairs an eerie scene was revealed. Artful Dodger Jr was sitting on the floor, head bowed. The Puppeteer was seated in a chair next to him as if she was trying to give him strength but felt unable to make physical contact with him. And standing to one side of the room was Farai's uncle, still in his bathrobe, one hand in his pocket. I can see it as if it were yesterday.

We carefully made our way into the room and sat down. As soon as we were seated Farai's uncle started to speak. He spoke with authority, truly like the elder of a clan that had lost its way. He firstly apologised to Farai and me, stating that a very disrespectful act had been perpetrated in our house. He went on to say that he was fast asleep when he'd heard someone rummaging in his things. He'd woken up to find the Artful Dodger Jr lifting his wallet from his briefcase. He said he had leapt out of bed and, grabbing his belt, whipped "this thief", who he then ordered downstairs. Now, as the uncle sat before us, he instructed the young man to confess to his crime and apologise for his disrespectful behaviour under a roof that had fed and sheltered him.

I cannot describe how I felt. The words "violated" and "dirty" just don't even begin to describe the confusing cloud of emotions that enveloped me.

The rest is a haze. All I can remember is that the Artful Dodger Jr stayed for a few more days and then left. Later, as mentioned, we learned that he had become a full-fledged accomplice to the Artful Dodger.

The Puppeteer one day, soon after this incident, confessed to me in a moment of weakness that her sons, her family, were cursed. She told me some fantastic story of how enemies of her ex-husband had put a curse on them and how ever since anything they touched would sour and rot. Yes, the Puppeteer had the gall to sit right in front of me and tell me that evil forces had turned all her sons into menaces of society.

However, the worst part was that, at this point, it all kind of made sense to me. There was definitely something very, very wrong with Farai's family and a curse did indeed seem like a possible explanation. By now, my reason had gone completely bye-bye and I was being pulled into the world of muti. I was beginning to believe.

Many years later, when I had finally left this crazy world behind, I received a message from Farai's uncle, congratulating me on my strength and telling me how delighted he was that—how did he put it? Oh, yes—"I was free from those who thought they had control of things."

I never heard from him after that, but he was the one redeeming factor in the incomprehensible drama that was life with the Sapienses.

4

What is the role of a manager?

Perhaps this is the question I should have asked when I so boldly made the suggestion that changed everything.

I reckon a manger is someone who solely looks after the interests of his or her client. A manager runs the client's diary, makes sure the right team of people are around the client and always has the best interests of the client in mind. They are paid to do that. Right?

In my insanity, because that is the only way I can describe my state of mind at this point in my life, I suggested to Farai that he become my manager due to his marketing background. It was beautiful—I had set myself the most wonderful trap and had opened the door Farai had longed to walk through.

Now Farai felt that he was the one in charge of the star everyone loved to hate. Any hope of making sense of my life, of maybe coming out the other end with a better handle on things, was dashed, by my own hand.

One of Farai's great talents was that he could talk the hind legs off a donkey. This often exhausted people to the point where they wouldn't actually hear or understand what he was saying but would smile politely while looking to me for rescue. He loved social gatherings and chastised me constantly for not having the time of my life at these pretentious affairs where we were all pretending we were the highest paid people in the world. It was a make-believe Hollywood, a Hollywood wannabe, and we all acted as if we were right there, having a ball in Tinseltown.

"Why?" I hear you ask.

We did not feel valued—as artists, as African people, as legitimate contributors to society at large. And nothing around us seemed to correct this. If we had looked a little more closely, we would have seen that we were treasured in the most important place of all—in the hearts of the people of South Africa and, I later came to learn, in the hearts of the African people as a whole. The ones who didn't have the power to buy us, the ones who just simply loved us for entertaining them on the screens in their homes, who were grateful to us for creating a world into which they could escape from the cruel and relentless challenges they faced every single day of their lives. That's who valued us. That's who surely we were doing it for. The photographs, the "glam" dresses, the red carpets and champagne glasses were a distraction. We did not need Hollywood gloss to legitimise who we were. We needed only to engage with the people of South Africa, but we were too in love with the idea of our own success to see this.

For me, these gatherings were torture. I am sure you have figured out by now that I really wasn't very good at being famous. Farai would constantly compare me with the other cast members, telling me how I should learn to "work" the crowd like they did. He also used to endlessly comment on my style of dress, basically telling me that I had no style. He would often talk of the young women he observed at these parties, who didn't have two cents to their names, but were "oh so well put together." There I was with all this money, and I had no idea what style was, was his constant refrain. I used to spend all day trying to put an outfit together, terrified that he would pull it apart. He always did, but in the most underhanded way. He would chastise me for always asking him how to dress, he would tell me to "surprise him", then he would rip my choices apart and literally be in my cupboard, pulling out clothes and creating my outfit for the night.

He would then huff and puff with mock frustration that I'd made him show me how to dress again. This was played out day in and day out.

There were times when he would even call friends who were designers and tell them to help me dress. Incredible! And I danced along like a puppet on a string. Hmmm . . . No wonder I called his mother the Puppeteer. Farai had learned from the best.

Every year he would organise an elaborate party on my birthday—the guest list made up of the who's who of Johannesburg.

One year he arranged a surprise birthday party with the help of his cousin who, yes, was also one of the lodgers in my house at some time or other in my relationship with Farai. Farai contacted a friend of mine who had a beautiful home in one of the affluent suburbs in Johannesburg and asked to use his home. He then invited all my "friends". When I look back at it, it is kind of disturbing. He had talent because he executed the plan beautifully, and from the outside it looked like something a devoted boyfriend—who wanted to do something really special for his lady—would do. However, on closer inspection, this was all for show. He wanted to make himself look good in front of all these people whose approval he so desperately craved. It really had nothing to do with my desires. If it had, it would have been a much smaller affair and far less expensive. It turned out to be pretty pricey, what with the caterers and so on. I think most people would agree with me when I say that I feel that the real surprise of a surprise party should not be how much it costs the person being surprised. This wonderful birthday gift made a huge dent in my bank account.

There I was, though, playing the oh-so-grateful girlfriend, and I was. I did not have the presence of mind to take a closer look and see what was actually unfolding.

Farai had bought into his *manager* role with aplomb, but when it came to having real conversations about my career, he bluffed his way through them. And he was proficient at it—bluffing, that is. So proficient that he almost convinced me that he was the one brokering the deals. He had some good ideas—don't get me wrong—but after a while he began to irk people in the industry. He "got in the way".

For many he was the perfect excuse to sideline me. So many of the megalomaniacs who controlled the industry wanted to see me "put in my place".

I had a conversation once with Farai, suggesting our lives had become too intertwined, that maybe he should get another job in the corporate arena. I claimed that my main reason for suggesting this was that despite what I was earning we kept running out of money. Admittedly, I am not very good at managing money, so I wasn't about to argue that this problem was solely due to taking care of his and his family's needs. But he was definitely helping me spend my money while at the same time complaining that he was working incredibly hard without being paid.

I never understood that statement when he made it, and he did, often. Even later on, when we were married and I was trying to divorce him, he tried to say I never paid him as my manager.

He should have started with the clothes in his closet, not to mention trips to the UK, Canada, Zimbabwe and Botswana, all on my dime.

We were both so deluded and our only solace came from chipping away at each other's sanity. There was no love, just a monstrous melodrama.

The relentless need to be bigger, stronger and better was the general terrain in which we lived and worked. That was South Africa for me in the late 1990s.

All that promise in April 1994, when I came to vote, to celebrate the victory that was South Africa, was being buried in "bigger", "better", "faster", "richer" and "badder". No one was looking to the future. It was all about now. The revolution was happening in the streets in the guise of violent crime, but it was also taking place in business arenas, including show business. The business I was in. The language of art had been buried, smothered, snuffed out.

5

I was still not married to Farai at this stage. This was six years into our relationship. Farai had proposed and had a ring made with money he'd had left from the last job he'd had in the corporate world. It was white gold with three diamonds running across it, linking a P in yellow gold to an F, also in yellow gold, surrounded by sapphires and rubies. It was unique and precious because it was the only thing he ever paid for with his own money during the course of our entire relationship.

My beloved father had fallen ill. He had lived ten years longer than predicted after having been diagnosed with prostate cancer, but the cancer was now spreading to his bones.

It was Christmas and my father desperately wanted a holiday. The doctors explained to him that, because of the chemotherapy, his bones were very weak and that travelling was not a good idea. Eventually they allowed us to take him to Knysna.

We drove to Knysna so that we could make the journey as slow and comfortable for my dad as possible. The first couple of days were wonderful. Sheila and I enjoyed the company of our parents—it was as if somehow the universe had allowed us to return to our idyllic youth, being on holiday with our wonderful parents, all other cares suspended for a couple of days.

Then it happened.

It was early morning when the phone rang in the hotel room and we heard the panicked tones of my beloved mother. All she could say was: "Dad fell! Come quick! Dad fell!"

We rushed into the room to find our father half-sitting and half-lying on the bathroom floor, one of his legs positioned at a strange angle. He was in agony and told us it felt as if something had snapped in his hip. Sheila and I called down to the front desk to request an ambulance. This was the beginning of the worst Christmas I have ever had. Even now, as I am relaying this chain of painful events, I can't help feeling a desperate anguish—it's as if it's happening all over again. It makes me wonder if in some instances we are perhaps doomed never to get over certain painful events in our lives. Maybe healing doesn't necessarily mean we forget. Did the families who lost loved ones in the apartheid era feel the way I do now every time they relive the details of the cruelties inflicted on their relatives, their sons and daughters? Do they feel the way I do now when they relive the last moments they spent with these individuals before their disappearances? The world said it was all over when the men in power said it was. For some it may never be over. Death, when it comes, in my experience, is impossible to get over. How much more when it is unjustifiable?

My father's hipbone had snapped and the doctors said that they would have to operate. He was seventy-seven years old, for goodness' sake! This would be a major operation. We spent every waking moment with him. He was always his vibrant, dynamic self and refused to give up.

I am going to share one last painful memory of this Knysna experience, and then I am moving on.

The morning of the operation, in the hotel that my mother, Sheila and I were staying in, we were eating breakfast, unable to even comprehend what was happening to us, when suddenly my mother collapsed. Sheila and I sat there helpless as we watched her shoulders heave up and down silently—her grief an open wound, bare for all to see because she was no longer able to hold it together. I had never seen my mother so helpless, and in that moment I prayed never to see it again.

The operation was successful. The doctors placed a pin in my father's hip to hold it together. He was then flown back to Cape Town in a helicopter ambulance, and, as soon as he had recovered sufficiently, was taken through various physiotherapy sessions. Ultimately, this powerful, brilliant son of Africa had to fight his last battles for his continent from a wheelchair.

It was during this time Farai suddenly asked to accompany me on a visit to my parents in Cape Town, where he asked for my father's permission to marry me. Farai decided to play the traditional African card by enquiring of my dad what my bride price would be. Farai's own prejudice against Africans he considered to be foreign clouded his ability to see the wisdom and the life experience he was confronting in my father. My father looked him directly in the eyes and his words were: "My daughter is not for sale."

He then proceeded to demand a signed prenuptial agreement. He declared that once he was presented with this legal document, signed by both of us, he would give our marriage his blessing.

The wind was somewhat knocked out of Farai's sail and he didn't mention marriage or the prenuptial agreement until I brought it up a few months after his encounter with my father.

My father's illness got the better of him and eventually he had no choice but to agree to being operated on again, as the pain from the metal in his hip was getting to be more than he could bear. Once that second operation happened, we had front row seats to my dad's life force being sucked back into the universe. All the time, he looked so beautiful. Even though he had the body of a malnourished child by the time he passed, he looked angelic. His crown of white hair sparkled and his fine, chiselled cheekbones were extremely visible, as all the flesh seemed to fade from his body. Cancer patients, I have heard, experience unbelievable pain as the cancer starts to rage, but my dad hardly complained of any discomfort. I was being forced to recognise that even death could be an infinitely profound experience when the one dying has lived his purpose and completed his life's journey.

This painful time was such a blessing. It was another opportunity to celebrate my father's life. I got to say goodbye to my dad, my best friend and my mentor.

In August 2000, at three am, my father passed.

This event seemed to mark a further low in the abyss that had become my life. It was as if all the negative forces in my world now gathered momentum. The Puppeteer was coming a lot more frequently and my house seemed to be filling up with all kinds of strangers, most of them connected to the Sapienses. Then one fine morning, as I was getting ready to go to work, Farai mumbled from the bed, his back to me, that he was having an affair. That he had been having this affair for quite some time and now he felt that he had to tell me about it because he was serious about this girl.

I felt for some strange reason that I had been shot. I am not even sure I loved Farai and yet I felt like I had been shot. How must it be for people who know they are in love? My legs would not move; I was numb all over. I just stared at him foolishly, the past year of our life together flashing before me. I saw myself spending stressful nights waiting for him to come home and waking up to the sun shining and the space beside me in our bed empty. I remember immediately crawling out of bed on these occasions, which were more than frequent, falling to my knees, hands clasped together in earnest prayer, begging God to bring him back home safely. This was Johannesburg—he could easily have been lying in a ditch somewhere, shot or maimed from a car accident or carjacking.

As the world spun back to this moment of hearing where he had been all those nights, I collapsed to the floor. I asked him who she was, as if that would somehow ease the unbelievable pain that was now ripping through my stomach and my heart. I felt unwanted. It was as if all my past experiences of being dumped or hurt by lovers had been rolled up into one sharp, poisonous arrow that had landed in the very centre of my being. Why couldn't I be worshipped? Why couldn't I be someone's dream partner? Why couldn't I be the type of partner never to let go of, the one to be treasured, the one to give thanks for every single day you are with them? I wanted him to love me unequivocally and have absolutely no desire to be with other people.

Was I unreasonable? Doesn't everyone want this?

What I hadn't factored in was that although I wanted this—to be worshipped, to be desired—this was not really the man I wanted it from because I didn't really connect with him. Our goals were different, our values completely opposite from each other, our life experience bore no commonality and I wasn't even attracted sexually to him—there was no chemistry between us.

Yet I wanted him to *love* me. Was it really from him I wanted, needed all that affection, respect and approval?

No, perhaps not. Somewhere in my life I had lost any sense that I—the self I was—was enough. What did that? When did it happen? How many others were going through it?

If I had paused on this last thought for a second, I may have handled things completely differently and come to recognise my purpose much, much sooner.

Eventually, I rose and left for work without saying a word.

6

She couldn't have been older than twenty-one. She was so small, so delicate. I was in my late thirties. I was full-bodied. Plump? Fat? I don't know.

I had the body of a woman. She was a girl.

I was a woman.

So why was I in this crazy position—having to force this "girl" off my partner like I was a teenager fighting for her boyfriend? Yet again, I resented the places I was being forced to go with this man. He just kept yanking my chain, forcing me to see how little I thought of myself.

Farai announced, soon after his confession of infidelity, that he was in fact a polygamist. He had fallen in love with this girl but he was not going to give me up because he loved me too, and therefore, in the tradition of true polygamy, I had to meet her. Why? Simply because he needed my stamp of approval. If I accepted her, having given her the once-over, she was to join our happy family and it would be my duty to teach her how to be a good partner to him.

I was not married to Farai at this point. I could have told him to pack his sick, twisted bags and leave my property. I didn't. I told myself that this was another little weasel entering Ntsiki's home, wanting to be her and she had found her ticket to that end in Farai.

I told Farai that his neat little polygamous scenario was not possible because I was a monogamist. His response was the same as the response I often received when I was appalled by something I just didn't understand: I was a foreigner and mentally colonised. I had lost touch with my African roots and was thinking like a white woman. Even the Puppeteer, a victim of adultery herself, had told me this. Her advice was that I should keep my mouth shut, cook for my husband, who wasn't even my husband, and do his bidding at all times.

There were countless days when I just wanted to take a gun to my head and pull the trigger. I, by the way, had conveniently forgotten the time I had slept with a man who had a live-in girlfriend. Is this what they mean by karma? Was this payback? Not from another human being but from the universe itself.

One morning, after another sleepless night when Farai had not returned home, I was staring out into space in the middle of my beautifully spacious garden, now knowing why he wasn't home, when the woman who cleaned my house came out to join me. She told me that she'd had a dream. In her dream a young, strange-looking girl was standing outside our front gate and begging to come in. The domestic worker said that her gut told her not to open the gate to this girl. The girl then swore at her and threw some leaves into the gate.

My domestic worker told me that this was muti.

I remember going cold—she had not seen Farai's young conquest and knew nothing of her. I asked her what she thought this dream meant. She said it meant that an intruder was trying to enter my home to disrupt it and it was imperative that I get protection. She said I needed protection from my ancestors, and, luckily for me, I had a very strong one in my father. I told her that I did not know how to do this, so she recommended a traditional healer from her church. Yes, this guy prayed to God, had Jesus as his saviour and used traditional herbs to ward off evil spirits.

It was at this point that I made the decision that I was going to prove my African authenticity at the deepest level, at the level of spirit. The fact that I was not familiar with this world at this point meant nothing. I needed allies and where better to get them than from the spiritual plain? Only which ones? Was it to be the angels in my head or the demons? I was about to find out.

I met with the high priest of what was called the "African" church in a rocky, remote part of Johannesburg (so remote, in fact, that if you were to ask me to point out its whereabouts today I wouldn't know where to begin). He took me to the highest rock and prayed over me. He then told me to sit and proceeded to tell me that I had the "gift", that I myself was a traditional healer. With this out of the way, he got down to business—there was an unwanted woman in my man's life and she was using traditional medicine to blind him. I would have to fight her on the spiritual plain to undo her spell. He then brought out two bags of herbs, one for my "husband" and one for me, and instructed me to stir a little into a glass of water and drink it every day. My "husband" was to do the same. This was imperative if I wanted him to be free. He had also written both of their names on pieces of paper and told me to burn them every day until the pieces ran out.

When I first approached Farai with what I had learned, he told me to go to hell, that I had lost the plot and that this muti was nonsense.

Interesting how we can pick and choose which parts of our African traditions are authentic and which are not. This communing with the ancestors, after all, was indeed a very African thing, as valid as polygamy, wouldn't you say? So we argued over which of these African traditions should be adhered to and which should not.

Human nature, right? We manipulate the data over and over again till it bends to our will. It was one hell of a battle, but I won—or at least I thought I had.

I was able to convince Farai that this girl was evil and had him under a spell. The turning point came when he insisted we meet.

I will never forget that surreal night. We sat in our dining room, around our dining room table, the three of us. I remember this girl looking at me in awe, posing away as she told me that she loved Farai and would be happy to accept being part of "our family". If I had been lucid, I would have seen a desperate young woman begging to be acknowledged, to be told she had some significance in the world. Instead, I fed the gaping hole in her spirit by giving her credence as my enemy, a worthy opponent. Can you imagine? She was now a part of *Generations*, for real. She was now at war with Ntsiki for her man. That was the truth of the matter, but I was as deluded as she was and unwittingly fed her fantasy by ordering her to get out of our lives.

Bursting into tears, she then explained that a relative was abusing her and she needed to get away from him. Farai supported her by saying we should allow her to stay with us until she could find her feet.

I looked at him as if he was insane, which, of course, he was. I refused.

I stated that it made no sense to allow the woman my partner was having an affair with to stay in my home. She cried, beautifully, but all I could see was the face of the young woman we had found sitting outside our house early one morning, claiming she had run away from home because of an abusive relative and needed "Ntsiki's" help.

I remembered the warning from the police that such characters wormed their way into your home then shouted rape and demanded compensation. Here she was again, in a different form, this time having climbed into my partner's bed. He was the weak link, and all the desperate vultures who needed "out" of their empty, wretched lives were gunning for him. But, then again, who could blame him? I had lost interest in having sex with him a long time before this. He had even accused me of having problems, of needing sex therapy. In his mind, I guess, I was worth keeping for the money and the fame, and then he could get someone else for sex. I think he was picturing his ideal life. A woman to have sex with, one to cook and one to bring home the bacon.

Farai and the lady in question finally left—he insisted on taking her home. I felt totally uneasy. As I mentioned earlier, my relationship with Christianity wasn't a good one, but I had taken to getting down on my knees and praying. This night, for the umpteenth time, I prayed for Farai's safety. Not long after this, I received a phone call from him saying that the car had broken down in the middle of nowhere and asking if I could please come and get him.

I ran down to the garage but for some inexplicable reason the garage door refused to open. I tried to put it on manual but it wouldn't budge.

This was the middle of the night.

I ran out to try and wake up a friendly neighbour and was greeted by their wild, clearly hungry dogs. I backed off, ran back to the house and got back on my knees. My mother always talked about getting down on your knees and praying when the going got tough. At this point, I finally understood my mother and her faith.

The phone rang again and Farai, clearly relieved, told me that a cop car had turned up out of the blue and all was well.

I thanked Jesus and resolved to tell Farai that this evil presence must be removed from our lives.

I discovered later that Farai had had meetings with the girl's mother regarding her being brought into our marriage as a second wife. The mother had agreed. She had agreed because that is how desperate poverty can make you. There is no knowledge of the fact that you can be your own source of creativity, your own source of wealth.

Strange events occurred when this girl was around, events I still cannot explain. Like the time Farai, a friend of his and I were racing down the motorway one night and Farai suddenly pulled over onto the hard shoulder, saying he felt there may be a problem with one of the tyres. We got out of the car and found that one tyre was completely shredded, as if some beast with talons had got at it.

We were all stunned. Farai's friend said that he had never seen anything like it. That day, my belief in dark forces and what they were capable of achieving was confirmed.

After that night, Farai listened and ended the relationship. The following day I insisted we get married.

Yes. That is what I did. I insisted, on that day, that this man, who had shown me he had absolutely no respect for our union by bringing a stray girl off the streets into my home, who wanted to be a polygamist, who had a family I had bankrolled for six or so years, marry me.

My father was no longer alive, so the prenuptial agreement he insisted on never materialised.

I was lost.

We booked a time and date that was virtually the next day. I invited my brother and his wife and one other friend. Farai's guest was the Artful Dodger.

Farai was unenthusiastic as he dragged himself to the Home Affairs office. He kept saying that he didn't know how he was going to promise to "forsake all others". I didn't know what to say. We had reached a stand-off. If he felt so strongly about his polygamous rights, there was nothing I could do about it and so I prepared myself for him to refuse to get married until this issue could somehow be resolved.

In reality, there was no way Farai didn't want the marriage—it meant more money and more fame. It would be all official. But I couldn't see this.

7

I remember the day of my so-called marriage like it was yesterday. I had, in the past, loved wedding ceremonies—they always looked so full of joy and celebration. My wedding day was dull and devoid of love and positive expectation. Everyone in the room either despised or was highly suspicious of one another. Farai was cold. I was jumping around like I had ants in my pants, consumed by a sense of utter discomfort. Come to think of it, I was never relaxed when I was around people in Farai's presence. I am ashamed to say I was always filled with a sense of dread and embarrassment. Imagine that: I married a man who I felt embarrassed to be around in public. Therapy. That is really what I needed. Not only had I married a man I felt embarrassed by, a man whose family I despised and mistrusted, but I had also married this man in community of property. My father must have been turning in his grave.

My career continued to soar and I continued to feel stifled by my own success. It was as if everyone else enjoyed my fame while I was consumed by a profound hatred of it. I basically had a problem with success, a deep-seated problem, and I spent every second of my life wishing it away.

You know, I recently saw an episode of *Superman* in which he meets this sorceress who can grant you your wish instantly. The point was that she tuned into your deepest desire at that moment and then asked you to make a wish. Superman's wish was just to be ordinary, to not have the mission he had and therefore have no knowledge of his power. That is what I was doing, and eventually I would get my wish. The power of thought. Beware.

It was as if getting married gave Farai permission to spin out of control. Meanwhile, it shrouded me in the feeling that I had deceived myself. Why had I insisted we tie the knot after so long? We had been together for six years without getting married. The conclusion I have come to now is one that fills me with dread and makes me squirm, because it says something about a deep-seated tendency I have, which has often meant I have fallen short of my goal. That tendency is the need to give away my power. I am consumed by the desire, sometimes consciously but more frighteningly unconsciously, to relinquish my ability to lead. I was trying to preserve a situation where I was unable to breathe, unable to express myself and where every resource I had—emotional, material, spiritual—was being siphoned out of me day by day, hour by hour, minute by minute. These are the actions of a victim. Victims are very powerful saboteurs of their own happiness. I was becoming a master at preserving my life in hell, and, as a result, hell was winning. Hell was becoming victorious!

Farai continued to come home in the early hours of the morning or actually more like somewhere in the middle of the day, having been out all night. It was on one of these days that he found me waiting for him in the garden. His eyes were red but with a strange twinkle behind them. He was in a very good mood but one that was rather unsettling. I told him, when he joined me, that I was leaving *Generations*. The man flipped out. He lectured me on how as my manager he strongly advised against this. I let him know in no uncertain terms that I knew my career better than he did and I needed to move on. I told him how every second I spent in the SABC meant a minute off my oxygen tank. I told him that the place was evil and that I felt some dark forces were tormenting me and making my life a living hell.

It was true in a way. I was not getting on with my producers and fellow cast members at all. I complained twenty-four/seven about the working conditions. I hated the fact that we were totally under management's thumb. We had no say in anything, it seemed. We were a product. I believed I was an artist, not a product. Well, this was a soap opera, it was a product, and anything associated with it was part of that product, that "brand". The language of business. I was a "brand", as Farai reminded me over and over, and the more I heard that word the more I wanted to scream my lungs out and run for the hills.

Where was Pamela in all this? I had a heartbeat. I had a pulse, a brain, and I obviously had some talent, otherwise I wouldn't have gotten myself into this mess by playing such a character so well! But I had no control and it was incinerating me. The irony is that I had no control because I had no vision, but, of course, I couldn't see this.

The upside of having control of one's life is that one becomes self-sufficient, confident and can create a wonderful tapestry for fulfilling one's goals. Negative controlling behaviour, meanwhile, comes from a lack of self-worth. Low self-esteem. Farai and I were on this merry-go-round into the pit of low self-esteem. His journey was much more dangerous than mine because it was in fact the only thing that drove him. He had a deep-seated hatred of himself and every action he took, I now see, was an expression of self-loathing. He had absolutely no respect for his life.

During this vicious discussion around my leaving *Generations*, it somehow came out that the night before he had been hanging around some people in the business, filmmakers and producers, and they were hitting the cocaine.

I told you how the South African film and television industry lived this delusional copycat Hollywood existence. Drug abuse was one of the terrible results of this bizarre scenario.

It was, and I am sure still is, a very serious problem. It got to the point where it began to claim the lives of young, talented people who just needed direction. My heart breaks when I think of those young talents. I curse Hollywood—it has done a great deal to mislead the burgeoning creative industries around the world. For some reason it isn't the positive practices of Hollywood that are adopted—it is the ugly, destructive practices that are emulated.

Cocaine makes you feel that you are invincible. It gives you a feeling of confidence that is bloated and erroneous. So you can imagine that if your deep-seated tendency is to feel worthless, cocaine must be like manna from heaven.

The problem is that everything you do comes from a place of aggression and the mood swings are dramatic—actions resulting from them more often than not are highly toxic and totally destructive. This is not a friendly drug.

I asked Farai if this was the first time he had taken the drug. It was not. Before walking away from him in the garden that day, I told him that if he were to become addicted I would leave him. I meant it.

I left *Generations* and began in earnest to try and bring some creativity back into my life. I had good one-off experiences with a number of shows, but none of the roles I played ever quite caught the imagination of the public in the way that my portrayal of Ntsiki had. The mass public. The faithful *Generations* following. It seemed difficult for the audience to grow with me and evolve.

Following this I had a couple of very painful episodes that would lead me to suffer a great deal.

One of them was a play I helped develop and direct. A young woman, who had been a student at the drama school I had taught at when I had first come to South Africa, had written a play and she wanted me to be in it. I read the piece and discovered there was no play. I told her that, instead of acting in it, I would be happy to help her develop it and ultimately direct it. She agreed and approached the Windybrow Theatre to give it a platform. They agreed.

As mentioned earlier, the Windybrow Theatre is situated at the foot of Hillbrow and audiences therefore hardly ever graced it with their presence. It was such a beautiful building and had such great potential to develop artists at grass-roots level, but it just didn't seem to be able to get itself off the ground. Here is where this young woman's play would be given a chance.

Now there is a problem when the people involved in a creative process are coming from a place of fear, anger and desperation. This young lady wanted recognition at all costs, but she wasn't willing to put in the effort. She somehow had convinced herself that she had written a play and because it had been performed at some festival or other she believed it was a complete entity. It wasn't. It was a shell of an idea. She wanted me to create magic with it and even be her voice but to somehow walk away with all the glory. You can imagine what transpired.

I managed to get fantastically well-known actors to agree to this project and during the rehearsals—rehearsals the young woman was invited to but never attended—we workshopped the play. At night, I would go home and write down whatever had come out of rehearsals that day. Eventually, I presented the young woman with what I thought was a wonderful, innovative piece. Unfortunately, she had been so busy acting the writer who never wrote, the writer who never attended rehearsals, that she had no idea what the story had become. And, as a result, when she was eventually interviewed by the press, she couldn't really answer questions about her play. The journalists then described this piece as something I had written and directed. I constantly tried to correct them, but they weren't interested.

The next thing I knew the young woman was attacking me, accusing me of stealing her work. It was absurd! I asked her to see reason—I really had no need to steal anyone's work. I had the platform and the skill, so why would I steal from someone who had potential but very little skill and no platform? She was too blinded by her own sense of inadequacy to see reason and walked away very angry and bitter, convinced I had tricked her.

The other ridiculous part of this project was that I had invited Farai on board as the marketing manager. I believed, having seen how he'd worked wonders with the nightclub years earlier, that he could get an audience into the Windybrow.

He did. It was a full house for opening night. But it was a full house for the opening night only. The play had a four-week run of empty seats.

I also had decided to be incredibly innovative and use what are called Intelligent Lights for my production, as the story was set inside a woman's head. The theatre management was terrified by my idea. I had directed at the Windybrow years before—a two-hander in which a white South African man and a black South African man engaged in honest dialogue about their true feelings about the "change" in the country. The play was received well, but people felt that the country just wasn't ready to witness this kind of entertainment on its stages. Now I was back and introducing Intelligent Lights. As you can imagine, I was not the Windybrow's favourite director.

The Intelligent Lights worked a treat, but they were too expensive for the theatre and they refused to pay for them. I paid for half out of my own pocket, but I couldn't fork out the rest. No audience, therefore no income. The Intelligent Lights people took me to court and even had bailiffs take my furniture because I couldn't pay. Eventually, I decided to join *Muvhango*, another SABC soap opera, and was able to pay off my debt and get my furniture back.

All of this left a bitter taste in my mouth and South Africa was beginning to look increasingly ugly to me. I felt that South Africa wanted everything I had to give without giving anything in return.

I was hitting rock bottom. I was being driven by all the negative emotions known to man. My soul was being grievously assaulted. I had this strange dream in the midst of all of this—I dreamt a lot, by the way, and they were often premonitions. This time I dreamt I was in some seedy, filthy club with tables strewn all over the place. I was weaving through this crowd of drunken clientele when suddenly, on the beer-splattered ground in front of me, was a young woman. She had very fair skin—she was "coloured", to use an apartheid definition of someone's ethnicity—and was staring up at me in a daze, high on alcohol or drugs. When she smiled there was a gap between her front teeth. Behind me, Farai whispered in my ear: "Meet my wife."

In the morning, I told him about the dream.

In the months that followed, I continued to work on *Muvhango*, a shadow of my former self. Then something quite wonderful happened. John Kani cast me in his new play *Nothing But The Truth* at the Market Theatre. The cast was formidable, what with John playing the lead and Dambisa Kente, one of South Africa's legends, being the other actress.

On hearing I was cast in this play, Farai announced he was having another affair. This was about three months after I'd had the dream.

8

With this new conquest, Farai was even more insistent that he had fallen in love and absolutely needed another wife. With this one, he was not going to hold back. I was going to accept that he was a polygamist, whether I liked it or not. I was going to share my wealth and success with his family, his wives and his lousy friends, and, gagging every step of the way, I did.

All I had to do was walk away, get a divorce and restart my life. Instead, choking and writhing with self-hatred, I soldiered on, trying to understand.

Farai brought this woman, who I will call Spike, right into the centre of our contaminated world. I was working in this mind-blowing, successful play, but I would return home every evening to what felt like black tar. I couldn't breathe. I couldn't see daylight. I started to smoke heavily. Sometimes, I would dash out of the house, away from the Puppeteer, who was now always there, and away from Farai's ailing brother who made it public knowledge on a perpetual basis that he was sick and dying and to hell with whatever was going on in our lives we were going to take care of him.

I won best supporting actress for my role in *Nothing But The Truth*. My career brought me recognition and even from those who hated me, respect. At home, those that benefitted from my labour treated me with complete disdain and a great deal of resentment.

Zindzi Mandela, one of the most beautiful, intelligent and vibrant people I have ever known, knew I had an interest in the spiritual landscape of my motherland. She always used to call me a "child of Africa", and I was always so infinitely grateful for that blessing. I still am. She, one fine day, told me where I could find Credo Mutwa.

This man I can only describe as a living oracle. When you Google his name, he is described as a "shaman, traditional healer, sangoma". Indeed, he is all these things—he is a spirit of Africa. When he goes, what goes with him is a wealth of African history and deep sense of the African character.

Funny, when I went to see him, he called me "Ntsiki".

At that time Credo Mutwa lived in a rundown dwelling in the heart of The Cradle of Humankind. Standing outside his abode I felt ashamed that as Africans we are so slack in the way we treat our treasures. Credo Mutwa is part of our African heritage and we were not taking care of him.

The earth is red in Magaliesberg; the mountains surrounding it are hard, slamming themselves against the blue African sky and wrapping themselves possessively around the valley below.

This is where Credo Mutwa lived.

He was so warm in the way he received us. I had taken Farai with me. Credo asked Farai what his surname was and then proceeded to give an extraordinary account of its heritage. I remember him saying that Farai was a descendant of those that had protected the leaders of the land. He gave him such respect, and when he finished telling him about the history of his name, he ended with: "I am pleased to know you, sir." It was quite wonderful. This man loved his continent and its people, and he knew everything there was to know about our psyche.

Credo told me that in 1994 he had asked to see the new government because he wanted to show them how to govern the land according to the African character. He argued that for us to continue to try and lead our country according to Western ideas, ideas alien to the African terrain, meant that we would always find ourselves at the mercy of others. He laughed when I asked him how he was received. He told me that they had refused to talk to him.

Credo then offered to throw bones for me. After throwing the bones, he chuckled and said I was a sangoma. He told me that I had inherited this gift from my mother, who was also a very powerful sangoma, and she had inherited it from an older woman before her, possibly my grandmother or great grandmother.

He then told me that I needed to dance to the beat of the drum. Moments later, he presented me with a red-and-white cloth.

After blessing it, he told me that my mother also needed to bless it so that I could begin my journey as a sangoma. I explained to him that my mother was a devout Christian and her spiritual guide was Jesus. He accepted this but said that she must, for the purposes of this journey, bless the cloth. I took it, feeling something very powerful and significant had touched my life.

Credo Mutwa chuckled again as he continued to read the bones. His words were: "You did not leave *Generations* of your own accord, you were pushed out by magical means."

I remember feeling stunned. There was a part of me that felt some kind of truth lay in this statement. It was a vindication of all those times I had felt as if the SABC building carried a very negative energy whenever I entered it. He made me feel sane in that moment.

Farai immediately jumped in and asked if it would be okay if I went back to Generations. Credo nodded. He said I would be fine; I was protected. I told him I had no intention of returning to the show, that I had moved on. He said that of course I was free to make any choices I wanted, but his request was that I get back on screen because role models were desperately needed.

That day was one of the best days of my life. It was like being suspended in time in some remote, secret part of the universe where I was somehow privy to a great revelation in the cosmos with all its wonder and mystery.

Thank you so much for the spirit of Africa, Credo Mutwa.

It was after that day that I decided somewhere deep in the core of my being that I was going to continue to search for my spiritual identity. That night, I wrapped the red-and-white cloth around my body and slept in it. I dreamt that I was dancing to the beat of the drum in some dusty compound. The drummers were female and I was stomping the earth, lost in the drumbeat. Finally, I fell into someone's lap. When I looked up it was Oprah Winfrey's face I was staring at. I woke up confused and totally disorientated.

The space beside me was empty as usual.

It was as if that visit to Credo had opened up a place in the universe with my name written on it. I say this because suddenly the spiritual language of South Africa in all its diversity became something I was desperate to explore, extensively.

Nothing But The Truth was going swimmingly. The director, Janice Honeyman, was quite wonderful and a master at dealing with actors and our egos.

Dambisa Kente had been very ill while we were touring the play but being the trooper that she was she never complained. She was just very weak and seemed to grow weaker as the run continued. It was when we came to do the final stretch at the Market Theatre, marking the end of the season, that Dambisa's strength failed her.

We'd rehearsed the play all over again for the run at the Market Theatre and had one last dress rehearsal to complete before the grand opening. I arrived at the time specified, only to be greeted by a series of panicky "Oh, my gosh!"s and "We've been trying to get hold of you!"s.

I was puzzled and somewhat irritated, since I was very much on time, but it quickly became apparent that the plans had changed. The last dress rehearsal was now to be a special performance for Nelson Mandela, as he wanted to see this play that seemed to be the talk of the town. And he had to see it that night because he was going to be out of the country for quite some time. This changed everything! I climbed off my superior chariot and proceeded to get on with getting ready.

My excitement was thwarted, however, by what I found when I rushed into the dressing room and saw a very weak Dambisa. I tried to persuade her to tell them she was ill and could not go on. She refused. Her argument was, as always on these occasions, that if she told them she was ill then when they took the play to England, which she had convinced herself was going to happen, they would not allow her to go. I assured her that this would not be the case.

Alas, she was not to be persuaded. And eventually the play did go to England without Dambisa and myself. Ironic.

Dambisa went on that night. We performed for Nelson Mandela and his small entourage of bodyguards and assistants.

Dambisa could hardly stand when taking the bow and then had to muster super-human strength when Tata Mandela asked to meet us after the performance. Sweat had started to pour down her face and I began to slowly panic inside as I realised something was seriously wrong. I remember hazily the two of us standing in front of this magnificent African hero who was so warm and generous with his compliments. I can hear his voice as he asked me which Nomvete I belonged to. I told him I was Bax Nomvete's child and he proceeded to tell me that my parents had taken care of him when he was in Ethiopia. This was the first time I had ever heard this. My parents had never mentioned that one of their many houseguests was none other than this legendary giant, Nelson Mandela. He then greeted Dambisa, thanking her for her own laudible contribution to South African theatre and film, and expressed how privileged and fortunate he was to see her in this play.

The next day, I received a call informing me that Dambisa had been rushed to hospital in the early hours of the morning and was critically ill. That night there was an emergency production meeting to figure out what needed to be done—the play was meant to open the following night. Much to my horror, there was a suggestion that we wait to hear what her condition was because she just might be able to perform on opening night. Then they would close the production and rehearse someone else for her part. Have you ever heard of such a thing? This girl had practically fainted on stage the night before, was rushed to hospital in the early hours of the morning and was described as being in a critical condition, and the production was actually considering dragging her out of bed to perform on opening night. I told the director I absolutely would not be part of such a callous plan. There are limits to the cliché "The show must go on." Even if an actress dies in the process? I don't think so. Luckily, it was finally agreed that we would postpone the show for a week and rehearse a new actress in the part. Nthati Moshesh was available for the role.

Dambisa Kente died a few days after being admitted into hospital.

A week or so later, John Kani announced to Nthati and me that Tata Mandela had asked that the three of us accompany him to Dambisa Kente's home to pay our respects, as he had been unable to make the funeral. While we all sat in one small room of Dambisa's family home, Tata Mandela spoke gently with her family, offering his gratitude for all Dambisa had done in the arts for the liberation of South Africa. Imagine how privileged I felt, how humbled to be witness to this most wonderful benison. This surely was the kind of leadership Credo Mutwa would have approved of. This was indeed the African way, where the king comes and honours his soldiers, encouraging the next generation to pick up the baton. It was beautiful and uplifting and filled with the promise of a greater tomorrow for South Africa and its people.

Tata Mandela then, out of the blue, turned to me and said: "Bax would have been so proud if he were still alive. Thank you for your performance in this play. He would have seen that you are a wonderful person and you are doing wonderful things."

I was stunned. On his deathbed, my father, when we were saying goodbye, had said those exact words to me. He'd said that I was wonderful and was going to achieve wonderful things. It was as if, at that moment, Tata Mandela had channelled my father's spirit to deliver this very important message. I was overwhelmed with the feeling that somehow I had better honour this instruction and fulfil my mission to make a difference. At this point, I had no idea how, only that my destiny had been sealed and I must not fail.

My encounters with Tata Mandela did not end there.

A few months after this, I got a call late one night from John Kani, telling me Tata wanted to speak to me. He gave me a private number and said I was to call him before seven the following morning. I was immediately on the phone to my mother. When I told her Nelson Mandela wanted to speak to me about something, she said that this was my father's doing. She felt he was trying to send me a message through Mandela. My mother always saw the true picture of all things whenever we were flummoxed by seemingly strange circumstances.

I didn't get much sleep and at five past seven the following morning I was on the phone to Mandela. I was greeted first by the voice of a very warm, matronly woman. She responded as if she had been expecting my call. A few minutes later I heard Nelson Mandela's voice on the other end of the line. It was surreal! For a second I thought it might be a prank—this voice that was so distinctive, calling me by name.

His next words had me keeling over.

He was inviting me to lunch because there was something he needed to discuss with me. He said that he knew *my* schedule was heavy, but if I could find *time* to see him, *he* would be *grateful*. We agreed on a date and time, but all I could think of as we did so was, foolishly, that I didn't know where he lived now that he wasn't president. I kept wondering how I would ask Nelson Mandela for his address. As if he could read my thoughts, he offered his address and extended his invitation to my husband.

I will not go into what my meeting with this most wonderful individual was about, but I will say he was incredibly humble and wonderfully magnanimous with his time.

This visit unravelled interesting aspects of my heritage as a Nomvete. I discovered that I had a determined uncle by the name of Mzuvukile that I learnt means "the house has arisen" in Xhosa. This uncle had an unshakeable respect for the Nomvete ancestors and had appointed himself their guardian. It also led me to meet another uncle of mine and develop a wonderful relationship with this man, now passed, who carried the same kind of strength and sophistication as my father.

Farai in Mandela's home, of course, rushed to pull out his camera so that we could record this momentous occasion. I mean, this is normal behaviour. Here was this man, this icon, and we were sitting in his house at his invitation—of course, you would want to record the moment by taking a simple photograph. However, I was embarrassed by his behaviour, and I kept wishing he wasn't there. So why, when Tata called to request my presence in his home for a second time, did I not leave Farai behind? It was as if I was powerless where Farai was concerned, as if my lack of respect for him consumed me with guilt and every action I took was an attempt at assuaging this feeling.

That second visit to Tata Mandela's sealed my deep respect for this man who was larger than life. The greatest thing about him for me was his humanity. As we finished off our lunch, a very important guest arrived and they were announced to him with the request that he receive them immediately. His words were: "They can wait. I am not finished here."

His message was loud and clear. It is not a person's status or social standing that commands respect; it is the simple fact that they are a human being.

A great leader.

And it stands to reason that a great leader leads a great country because he is of its people and therefore carries their spirit and they carry his.

I so wanted to believe that of South Africa and its people.

9

Zulu Love Letter, directed by Ramadan Suleman and written by Bhekizizwe Peterson, followed hot on the heels of *Nothing But The Truth*.

I had been called for this unusual audition. I say "unusual" because we were asked to improvise. The improvisation was a woman's reaction to hearing that her husband is having an affair with her sister. She wasn't my sister, but every single day I was reminded that this woman was in my husband's life. The fact was that Spike claimed that she loved the idea of being part of a polygamous structure and had written me several letters begging me to meet with her. So, for me, this audition came from the heart. Funny, as I was going through it, the lights went out. There was a brief power cut!

I remember Bheki saying that my audition was so powerful that it affected the electricity. We all laughed but now, as I look back, my emotions were so charged that it probably was the force of them that plunged us all into darkness. After all, that was now my dwelling place. I was living in the dark. *Literally.* I used to look around me in envy at people as they were carrying on with their lives, going about their daily routine. I hated my life. I felt stifled by it. I would often don the red-and-white cloth Credo Mutwa had given me when the house was full of Sapienses, hide myself in my bathroom and lie on the cold marble tiles. I used to stay like that for hours. It was the only spot only spot in my environment I felt I could lay claim to.

I was so grateful for all the work I was getting. I needed it. It became my solace, and because I was off the television screen I could focus on my craft as an *actress* and not get caught up in the trappings of being a *celebrity*.

After some weeks, I heard through the grapevine that the producers of *Zulu Love Letter* were looking for actresses in the UK and the US. I was furious. This made no sense. I had built a career, an illustrious one in the UK and now in South Africa, and the bonus was that I was a South African! To some, a foreign South African, but a South African actress living in South Africa nonetheless. I hadn't even been given a script and had heard that the actresses who had been approached in Europe and the US were afforded that luxury. Later, I discovered they had approached very well-known actresses, which means they were going down that understandable but still most painful route of casting an international star.

I fought for this role. I felt it was mine. Getting it, I decided, would send a message to the South African film industry that we could create a subculture of movie making that promoted local talent. I believed—and I still believe—that this will bring us true recognition on the global stage.

Finally, after several meetings with the director where I told him I was the right person for the role, I was called in for a screen test. And I am pleased to say that the only other actress I was up against was a fellow South African. I got myself an acting coach—ironically enough a young man from Zimbabwe, who I had met through a contact in the industry. He was amazing and I honestly attribute getting the job as well as my performance in the film to the work he did with me. People didn't like his presence on set, but I needed him.

This was a very demanding role. People marvel at American actors and their performances, but the level of support they get off screen is second to none. They are so prepared that they would have to be the worst talent in the world not to shine. I needed him. As I said, this was a demanding role.

I will never forget that at the Venice International Film Festival a woman came up to me after the screening and asked how *Zulu Love Letter* had been received back home in South Africa. Alas, I had to tell her it hadn't even been screened there yet. Europe was the first port of call. What a horrendous experience that was! It was a moment of heartbreak for me.

And unfortunately it wasn't the first moment of heartbreak and was very far from being the last.

It had begun with Farai. Okay, so my husband/manager who wasn't really my manager was an appendage, but still I shouldn't have been made to feel that taking him along to the film festival was a "problem". They made me feel my demands were unreasonable. I wasn't inviting an entourage; I was asking to be accompanied by my husband. Frankly, their opinion of him was irrelevant.

It had continued when we had arrived in Venice. I had been all dolled up for the press conference, but by the time I got there, because we had to take the local bus—the support team could not even afford a taxi, for goodness sake—I was sweating and panting. My hair was out of shape and my mascara had run down my cheeks, leaving me with two black rings around my eyes. I looked a mess and my feet were killing me. And so it was that "the star from Africa" hobbled into the press conference.

It was mad, come to think of it. If only I had understood that every single thing in my environment was reflecting the low opinion I had of myself back at me. It would have changed everything.

I later learned something wonderful. Bhekisizwe Peterson, the writer of this most wonderful project, *Zulu Love Letter,* told me at the wrap party that when they had gone to England they had quickly discovered how well respected I was as an actress there. He also said that one of the actresses they were looking at was Marianne Jean-Baptiste, who had won a Golden Globe for her role in *Secrets and Lies* and is now one of the leads in the American TV show *Without a Trace.* She had expressed a keen interest in the role but had asked if they were looking at any South African actresses for it. When they told her that yes, one of them was an actress called Pamela Nomvete, she told them she knew me well and that we had worked together, which we had in a three-person play some years previously. She apparently told them that they couldn't cast a better person as in England I had been one of the actors the black artists looked up to.

I was overwhelmed with gratitude but couldn't help feeling disappointed that it took the "approval" of a well-known English actress to give the producers the confidence to cast me, when I was a successful South African actress. Their "bravery" was vindicated when I won best actress at the Fespaco Film Festival in 2005. Meaningless in South Africa, but in Europe it is seen as a great achievement.

The award is something I treasure and before I die I pray I win a few more awards at Fespaco. African pride is a must, don't you think? I think this is what Credo Mutwa was trying to tell us.

I loved that film, and my wonderful co-star, young Mpumi Malatsi, won best actress at the Durban International Film Festival. At least *Zulu Love Letter* received some recognition in South Africa. I understand the film did not go down well at home. Why? Perhaps it lacked the Hollywood ingredients: violence and sex.

Those films are fine, but it is time, I think, South Africa made room for films on pure artistic merit as well. Other African countries have done this and made a huge impact on world screens without compromising their African integrity—all without the Hollywood stamp of approval. Just an opinion, but I hope one that is shared by many.

Every day I went in to rehearse for *Zulu Love Letter* I would stare at a beautiful poster, a poster for the film *Lumumba*, directed by Raoul Peck. I had seen this film some time before and expressed a deep desire to work with its director. I longingly stared at that poster, amazed that it was covering one of the walls of the building I was rehearsing in. As I mentioned earlier, we cannot underestimate the power of the mind, because almost a year later I was cast in *Sometimes in April*, a film by Raoul Peck that was produced by HBO. This film reawakened me to the reason I chose to be an actress.

This all sounds wonderful, doesn't it? Dreams coming true, getting cast in projects I wanted to be in. African stories.

Well, it was all horribly marred by the fact that away from the film sets I was sitting opposite Spike in restaurants, trying to understand why I was sitting there. On occasion, Farai was there and the whole time we were discussing the ludicrous subject of polygamy.

No offence to those who practise it and are happy with it, but to me it was absurd. There was absolutely no place for it in my life, so why was I willing to engage in this very bad, third-rate drama? You know what, no one will believe me, and I accept that, but the truth is I really wanted to understand. If this was some integral part of African culture, I wanted to understand.

The one person who knew that was Farai, and he manipulated this need of mine to "understand" to suit his own ends. Let's look at this from his point of view:

I was a public figure. Ntsiki, when she was on the screens, had almost cult status. To be honest, even off the screens, she was adored. Here you are, the guy that married her. You rise from being Joe Bloggs to being a superstar overnight, simply by being in the right place at the right time. Your means to that end seems to lose interest in you as a man, and yet she gives you absolute freedom with her bank accounts, her home and her cars. Sweet. You are free to basically do whatever you want. Farai once told me, when he was clearly very high on cocaine, that women threw themselves at him now in a way they never had in his entire life. He actually told me it made him feel like nothing because he knew they didn't want him for him, they actually wanted me or my life. He put it far more crudely: "They only want to f*** me because they want to f*** you," he once said to me.

For some reason, he made himself believe that Spike was different and wanted him for *him*. I once told him that I would one day leave him and that when I did his house of cards would fall. Spike would leave him because her "fix" would no longer be available—all this Tinseltown nonsense that came with *my* success would go with me—and he would die very lonely and probably penniless.

Actually, I think deep down he knew this was true, but he needed to believe he hadn't completely disappeared. Fame feeds your delusions if you have no idea what to do with it. You are given God status. People believe you hold the key to their happiness. Frightening.

You do actually have to employ superhuman efforts to set that record straight and keep your feet on the ground. Neither Farai nor I was equipped for it and consequently we were drawing our collective destructive energies into its vortex.

What is so disturbing about all of this is that it all happened on a subconscious level. I could only see what had actually happened years later when I came back into the land of the living and got back on track with my life.

When I was twenty-five, a clairvoyant told me I should stay away from drugs because they would destroy me. He told me I would have a nervous breakdown and it would be a waste of time because I would take years to build myself back up again. I didn't understand what he was talking about at the time because I have never found drugs appealing.

He didn't tell me that the drug was called "fame and money". He was right. I did crash in the end and it has taken me some time to put Humpty Dumpty back together again. But he was also wrong. It hasn't been a waste. Not one little bit.

10

Life can be so strange. It had gotten to the point where Spike was now spending weekends at our house. Picture this: the three of us watching films in the television room together. Farai was on one side of the room and Spike and I were on the couch but sitting as far apart as we possibly could. What was going on? I remember Farai once said how ridiculous it was that when he was alone with either one of us, we were all over him physically, but as soon as the three of us were in one room we behaved like strangers. Who was this guy?

One weekend, Farai and Spike arrived at the house looking like cats that had got the cream and told me that they wanted me to experience some of the joy they got from the drugs they took. This particular night they wanted me to try this "really harmless drug" called Ecstasy. We all know this drug and we all know just how "harmless" it is. Kids have thrown themselves under buses while high on this stuff and had heart attacks and other complications. This is a killer. Nothing harmless about it.

After relentless coaxing I agreed to try half a pill. It was the worst experience I have ever had. The sensation was horrible. My body temperature dropped dramatically. I felt cold and clammy and at the same time I had this weird tingling sensation all over. Constantly. The next day I felt depressed and angry. I told them that it was horrible and that I never wanted to do it again. They never asked me to.

You know what?

It was disgusting. This whole thing. I reckon Farai's intention was eventually to have some kind of music video scenario with drugs, alcohol and a nice little threesome. Hah! Over my dead body. Call me old fashioned, but I prefer two in a bed all the way. My idea of sexual adventure? Exploring tantric methods of lovemaking or maybe even the Kama Sutra, reaching a state of heightened consciousness through lovemaking with my partner. Just him and me!

After this, I couldn't be in the house when Spike was around. I was constantly exiling myself from my home as I accommodated all Farai's needs. I was the most visible person in the house, outside it. Yet, inside it, I seemed to be taking every action to be invisible. It was like I was ashamed of my success. It was as if I felt I needed to share my fame because I knew I wasn't entitled to it. This phenomenon is hugely misunderstood. The fame game is simply too much to cope with on one's own. I guess I believed I just wasn't large enough to handle it. Put even less succinctly, my life force wasn't large enough to handle it. Or so I believed.

11

When Raoul Peck cast me as Martine, the schoolteacher in *Sometimes in April*, I thought I was going to explode. This was truly a dream come true. Even better, we were shooting in Rwanda, after spending a week rehearsing in Paris. I was to be out of the house for a month and a half. Freedom!

This was an HBO film and the lead actor was Idris Elba, then the star of the popular American series *The Wire*. It sounds like my big break, doesn't it? After this kind of exposure, you'd think that that would be it. Finally, I was on the map! It was huge for Idris Elba. You all know him, and he works constantly. For me, it was almost like the beginning of the end.

It opened a door, but somehow, behind it, there was only a brick wall, a wall that knocked me down and gave me semi-permanent brain damage.

When I stepped off the plane I don't think I exhaled for at least twenty minutes. Rwanda is one of the most beautiful countries I have had the privilege to visit. The climate is slightly humid. The land is a combination of robust lush green mountains and red-stained earth. By the time I left my skin looked like I had just been for the best, most expensive facial money can buy.

We were given a great deal of time to research the genocide and as we were staying in Kigali many of the memorial sites were easily accessible. The lead actress in the film was from Rwanda and she very kindly acted as our guide on many occasions, as did the other Rwandan people I met during my stay.

When speaking to people about their experiences in Rwanda it was always overwhelming. One of the strangest aspects was that the harrowing tales of human cruelty and endurance we heard were often told to us by people who showed little or no emotion. I was consumed by a sense of horror and wonder. A million Rwandan men, women and children were slaughtered in those hundred days in April 1994. Here we were, ten years later, shooting a movie to tell their story, with all the memorial sites as references. It really felt as if we were reliving those hundred days. I could feel the agony of those souls in those lush green mountains and through the red soil that perhaps was stained with their blood.

For the first time in my what was then nineteen years acting experience I did not need to draw on my skill to tell the story. I was immersed in it and all I had to do was just be. This was a pure heart communication.

I was reminded of what drew me to my profession in the first place. The oh-so-simple desire to make a difference.

Every day I was on that set was absolutely wonderful. The time off was equally exhilarating, as cast and crew discussed the importance of the work we were doing. We, from many different countries and backgrounds, were all reminded of how precious the human spirit actually is.

When I was back in my hotel room, Farai would call me, and all I did every night was beg him to get Spike out of my house and my bed. He would lie to me, saying that while she was there in our house, me being away and all, she was sleeping in the spare room.

I wished my life away, fantasising about what it might be like if I didn't have this unwanted element back home. I was so much happier being in a hotel room in a strange country, working. This was my sanctuary. I was far more comfortable reliving a devastating episode in human history than I was in my "normal" life. Being on the phone with Farai made me want to eradicate the human spirit from the face of the earth. You can imagine the crazy internal warfare raging in my soul.

Raoul Peck insisted on shooting *Sometimes in April* in Kigali when HBO was considering South Africa. He also insisted on premiering the film in Rwanda. He felt he could not take *Sometimes in April* to the world until he had the approval of the Rwandan people. This he got.

Mr Peck had a screen put in the main stadium in Kigali. He had two people translating in Kinyarwanda, one of the indigenous languages of Rwanda, on microphones. When we arrived on the afternoon of the premier, the line of people waiting to enter the stadium snaked its way from the entrance to practically the centre of Kigali. People had come from all over the country to see this film.

Sitting in our seats, we were mesmerised by the spectacle before us. People were literally jumping over fences, pouring into the stadium from every possible entrance. Various people with megaphones were on the field, trying to maintain order, one of one of those people being Raoul Peck, the director!

It took two and a half hours for the crowd to settle and in the end the stadium was so full that people had to sit on the field itself, directly in front of the magical screen that was about to tell their story.

When the film began, a hush fell upon us. I kept my eye on the people on the ground. Nobody moved a muscle for three hours. I have never seen anything like that, ever.

Fifteen minutes after the end of the film the stadium was empty; the crowd had left in silence.

Driving to our after-party, we noticed the whole of Kigali was silent as people walked back to their homes. At the party, many Rwandan guests said to us that for the first time they felt that their story had been told. They told us that it didn't matter if it won an Oscar; the film would remain in the hearts of the Rwandan people. And they hoped that those who watched it would finally hear their voice and ensure that such a thing never happened again. Anywhere in the world.

I had wanted to invite my agent and the then first lady to the premier of this film, but when I suggested these additions to the guest list I was treated as if I had made the most unreasonable demand imaginable. Everyone else was coming from Europe or the US (flying first class, I learned later). I was travelling economy from South Africa, just around the corner, and yet my simple request that these individuals be allocated tickets to see the opening in Rwanda was dismissed flat out. I can't help wondering if this was because to them I was just an actress from South Africa and therefore should have known my place and sat quietly in abeyance, eternally grateful to be given any opportunity at all.

Despite this somewhat sour ending to the project, I was grateful to have been part of the telling of a true African story that honoured the beauty and resilience of my people. It wasn't the job that gave me a new perspective on my profession, per se, it was what it stood for that counted.

I wish the same kind of circumstances had surrounded *Zulu Love Letter*.

I left the *Sometimes in April* experience feeling that things would never be the same again. I knew I had to make some serious decisions about my life.

This was all to be put on hold, however, because as soon as I arrived back in South Africa Farai and Spike decided to turn up the heat. It began as soon as I landed. I was picked up at the airport by *both* of them! The wonder of Rwanda, the feeling of "making a difference" and the joy of basking in the wonderful craft of movie-making were wiped away in one fell swoop. They had decided that we were all going to go for a therapy session, so we could work out how to give Farai what he wanted. A polygamous relationship. I didn't want that, and neither did Spike (despite what she said), but now we had declared war: she was going to beat "Ntsiki" and I had accepted the challenge. What was I fighting for? It appeared to be Farai, but it was in fact my pride. Pride, a terrible flaw in the human psyche. And so, off I went to therapy with Farai and Spike.

The therapist, a woman called Hilda, was absolutely wonderful. She was not a regular therapist but what I can only describe as a spiritual therapist. She looked at one's situation holistically by examining the reasons as to why one might find oneself in a predicament and identifying what Buddhists would describe as a karmic tendency, patterns that might be the cause of one not being able to break free from a particular mode of behaviour.

Interestingly enough, Farai found her. A Hindu practitioner Farai had bumped into on one of his escapades had introduced her to us. This woman, when she had first met Farai, had pulled him aside and told him that he suffered from chronic low self-esteem and, if he chose, she could help him. So when Farai and Spike insisted we go to therapy to help sort out our mess, instinctively I said the only person I could trust, who I believed would be objective, was Hilda.

In her sessions, we were first required to do breathing exercises and perform a mild form of meditation, and then and only then would she start the session. We didn't seem to make any progress in terms of our views on polygamy and the crazy situation we were all involved in, but Hilda unlocked something that made me want to go even deeper into the reasons I had found myself in a love triangle.

Spike made what I found to be an unbelievably irritating comment during one of our sessions. She stated that she found it extra-ordinary that I allowed her to stay in my house and was even willing to engage in conversation with her because there was no way that she would even have contemplated doing these things if it had been the other way around.

Hilda very kindly came to my defence and said that the reason I was able to do this was because I was "enlightened".

Yes.

I almost burst out laughing. In fact, I probably would have if I hadn't been seething. How could she admit such a thing? Why the hell was she doing this if she would have found it offensive were it her husband and her life? Perhaps what I should have been asking myself instead was why I was letting this happen if this was indeed love?

If you are in love with someone, would you not then do everything in your power to make sure nothing threatened your relationship?

Or is that ownership?

When Hilda described the dysfunctional nature of our relationship, she said that Farai and I were codependent. This is a totally inappropriate form of relating to someone else. It is, in fact, a cycle of abusive behaviour. In our case, Farai needed me to boost his self-esteem and support him and his family financially. In return, I needed him to boost my own self-esteem, by being needy, and feed my desire to feel indispensable and therefore in control of my life.

Hilda said that what we needed to work towards was becoming interdependent. This is when two people have their own unique qualities and are clear about their individual purpose, then engage in a wonderful dance, supporting each other and building a safe haven that allows them to grow and expand as they discover and unveil their full potential.

Come to think of it, this was probably one of the reasons I could not handle fame. My relationship with my fans was a mirror of myrelationship with Farai. I wanted them to find me indispensable but at the same time I hated their need to take possession of my life. They left me feeling persecuted and acting the martyr. The platforms I found myself on could have been used to encourage others to tap into their own potential. Then I would have been in control of my life, through being clear about my purpose and the vehicle I was going to use to achieve it.

How come I hadn't figured this out earlier? What was it that blocked me from seeing and living my real life?

Delusion.

I was blinded by my own inability to believe in my potential. Like most of us, I was hell bent on proving how inadequate I actually was. Low self-esteem. It is a disease.

Farai's method of self-destruction, due to his own low self-esteem, was going to be through drugs or sex or maybe, once he had created enough scenarios confirming his being a waste of space, taking his own life.

Hilda explained to me, when I began to go to her on my own, that Farai needed physical assistance to help him repair his life as well as therapy sessions. She suggested yoga or meditation because a kind of metaphysical change had to occur from within—he had suffered, she claimed, some kind of severe trauma in his past that he was totally closed to and his recovery depended on him unlocking it. Hilda added that without this physical assistance Farai would eventually kill himself by either committing suicide or creating situations in his life that would cause his death.

Farai refused to take Hilda's advice. I guess he found it hard to believe that his background—an abusive childhood, dysfunctional family, poverty—did not have the power to hold him back from becoming a truly productive member of society.

On the occasions I went to Hilda on my own, she took me through a process called "rebirthing".

This process was designed to open up in me the ability to nurture myself. Through it, she identified that I, on observing my father living his purpose against all odds, had developed this need to protect him from those who I felt did not give him the recognition he deserved. I somehow had created a scenario in my head that I, and I alone, would make sure Dad received the respect that was long overdue.

Hilda told me my father was absolutely recognised where it counted and he wanted me to know this.

She told me that she could see him sitting around this banquet table on the other side, with all the other heroes who had lived, and that he was content with what he had achieved in his life. He wanted me to find my own purpose and be hugely successful in achieving my own goals.

Unfortunately the fantastic progress I was making with Hilda was halted abruptly because the situation at home was becoming more and more demanding and my finances were depleted. I had to stop the therapy midstream.

Hilda's last piece of advice to me was: "You are on the train towards living your potential. Farai at the moment is on the platform. You mustn't feel the need to get him on the train. It has to be his decision. Whatever you do, don't get off to persuade him to join you. You must keep moving because the train is gaining speed and you can't afford to wait."

Amazingly insightful, don't you think?

I now believe that you can take people onto that train, as a way of showing them the possibilities, but we are not responsible for what they do with that information when they get it.

Farai and I were definitely going in different directions. We just were too far gone to see what was coming and lacked the wisdom to stop it.

12

Farai found a cheaper way for us to work through our problems. He found a sangoma in the heart of Soweto. This man seemed a nice-enough guy but he was not Credo Mutwa. At this point, all reason had left the saga that was now my life. I was clutching at anything that might give clarity, perspective, anything that might show me the way. This sangoma's dwelling was two tin shacks. He seemed fairly popular because every time we went there was always a queue of people waiting to see him.

The first visit was very interesting in that the sangoma confirmed two things Credo had read in the bones. This took away any scepticism I may have had about the revelations that came from the sangoma's bones. He told me I had the gifts of the sangoma. He was so adamant about this that he refused to take money from my hand, as he claimed I was a "child of God". This did not mean that the session was free, though. No. He would only take the money from Farai's hand.

The second thing he said was that I had been pushed out of *Generations* by "magical means".

This gentleman then proceeded to bathe me in a tin bath full of herbs for protection and make strange incisions on my body with a razor blade. After he had finished, he chuckled and said he couldn't wait to see their faces when I returned to *Generations*.

Farai looked thrilled at this possibility as I secretly reinforced my vow never to return to that show.

Now, when I look back, I can see how far gone I was, because I never even stopped to consider the hygienic implications of what I was doing. Razor blades? I never checked to see if he had disinfected them. Child of God or not, something was definitely protecting me.

The sangoma then told me that my ancestors wanted me to go to Bulawayo in Zimbabwe and talk to the mountain. He explained that at certain times of the year people from all over went to a famous mountain in that region to commune with their ancestors (and the mountain would talk back to them). At this point, nothing appeared more absurd than the situation I was living in, so mountains that talked were a breath of fresh air and I was ready to have a go.

He further explained the amount of money I would need and also told me to take along a bottle of white spirit as an offering. The ancestors, it seemed, had a penchant for alcohol.

This was all very strange because my mother's relatives were direct descendants of King Mzilikazi, King Shaka's archrival. The story goes, after much acrimony, he eventually broke away from Shaka and headed towards Zimbabwe during the time of the great trek in the nineteenth century, settling in the northern part of the country.

Apparently, the name Bulawayo originates from Nguniland, that was once occupied by the Khumalo people. My mother's maiden name was Khumalo.

In Bulawayo, one of the languages spoken, Ndebele, is a cousin to Zulu, as a result of this fascinating history, the fight for power and wealth. The story of all human history.

With all these seeming links to Bulawayo, how could I not at least investigate the possibility of actual dialogue with my ancestors from my mother's side, the side that Credo had credited with spiritual know-how?

Farai was from Harare and was Shona, probably rivals to the Ndebele people, as I understand Bulawayo houses the strongest opposition to Mugabe's government (Mugabe also being Shona). I also found it interesting that I had some links with Farai's country of birth.

The stage was set, and Farai decided he was definitely going to accompany me on this journey. Perhaps he felt it might explain a few things about his place in the world.

A week before we left for Bulawayo I had a strange dream, having fallen asleep on my bathroom floor while wearing my red-and-white cloth. In the dream I found myself in the middle of nowhere. The land was arid and the African sun was beating down, relentless in its intensity. Two people—a young man and a woman—and I were sitting on the side of a rocky mountain and dangling our feet. Suddenly, I looked up at the cloudless blue sky and it opened up right before my very eyes and rays of light came pouring out, followed by a procession of livestock. Cows and sheep with bells around their necks were falling from the sky, crashing into the ground all around us.

I stared in awe, but when I tried to share my wonder with my companions they claimed they could not see what I was seeing. To them the sky was blue and still—no rays, no procession of cattle.

I told them that they were insane. I urged them to look harder, and, as I said this, I pointed out a cow that had just fallen next to one of them. Still they saw nothing. Eventually, the young man stood up and started to make his way down the mountain. I warned him to look out for wild dogs. He pooh-poohed my concern and continued his descent. A few minutes later we heard his scream. I scrabbled to my feet. The woman simply shrugged, stating it was his fault—I had warned him, after all.

It was then that I woke up.

I had driven with Farai many, many times to Harare. The kerfuffle at the South Africa/Zimbabwe border was always strenuous. When crossing one had to try to get away with taking cans of petrol over the border as there was always the possibility you wouldn't find any on the other side. The red tape around this alone was enough to drive you to commit murder.

I would often think of my dad's vision for a united Africa on these occasions, feeling that it really shouldn't be this hard to go across a line and visit another country on the same continent. I also used to find these trips harrowing because we would need to get foodstuff for various members of Farai's family across as well. This was a nightmare because not only did it take hours to get whatever it was through the border, but it meant having to sit with umpteen relatives who would reiterate over and over how difficult their lives had become. These were doctors, teachers and businessmen who now lived in one-room houses when apparently they had owned grand homes. Then would come the demands for money, which we would have carried with us in American dollars. These trips were always so draining both on my spirit and resources.

This time was different.

I know this sounds incredibly self-centred, especially given people's circumstances, but I couldn't help feeling this way. No one was going to take anything from me.

Also, the scenery was different from what I had gotten used to when driving to Harare. The landscape was rich with vegetation. It was green and had a magical quality about it, which was quite eerie at times. It felt as if there were some very important secrets hidden in the trees and the ground on which they stood.

The night fell upon us suddenly as it does in Africa and the landscape took on a gloomier persona. I was getting very nervous and thought that this was absolutely the kind of place where the mountains would speak. Farai started to express concern about our whereabouts, when suddenly two wild dogs ran out in front of the car's headlights. They were like guides. I expressed this to Farai and instructed him to follow them. He did so, and when they disappeared we found ourselves in front of a kraal-like structure. It was pitch black and the silence that enveloped us was thick with expectation.

As we adjusted to the dark we noticed a fence made up of tree branches and behind it was a series of mud huts. We searched for an entrance to this compound, feeling that we had no choice but to wake one of the occupants in one of the huts. We knocked tentatively on the wooden door of the hut nearest to us and were greeted by a male voice that shouted out as if sounding an alarm. Luckily for me, Farai spoke a bit of Ndebele and responded, reassuring the man that we came in peace. That was another talent Farai had: he spoke four or five African languages.

A young man stumbled out to us and we explained that we had come to converse with the mountain and were in fact looking for the gatekeeper.

He told us that we would only be able to get to him in the morning. The only option we had was to spend the night inside their yard in the car.

I was humbled by his hospitality, considering we had crashed into his world in the middle of the night.

Cowbells and sheep bleating were my alarm.

I tried to shift, having spent a very uncomfortable night in a strange position in the car. The glare of the sun was particularly unforgiving, so it took me a while to open my eyes and focus on my surroundings. Yes, we were definitely in a kraal. This compound contained modest dwelling places for the humans and a section for the livestock.

As I hauled myself into a sitting position, I was able to get a fuller impression of our surroundings. We were in a kind of valley. I say "kind of" because valleys, one imagines, are green and lush. This was rough, rocky terrain and the mountains that enveloped us were jagged, unsympathetic.

As I focused I was overwhelmed by a sensation that I can only describe as recognition. This place was familiar to me! For a moment I was in a total state of confusion because, as I examined the livestock, with bells dangling from their necks, the feeling grew. I knew this place! This was the place of my dream, the one where the sky had opened up and started raining cows and sheep with bells round their necks. Hilarious!

As the day unfolded I was consumed by the idea that I was onto something big in terms of my own personal relationship with the land and its spirits in relation to my heritage.

Having bathed under the open sky, we followed our host, clambering over rocks and small, rocky hills while looking nervously over our shoulders, as our guide had warned us of the presence of wild dogs. Yes, my dream, even down to the wild dogs!

We finally reached a wide-open space with a convenience store at one end and a dilapidated bar at the other. People were scattered around, lying on the ground, barely shaded from the fierce sunlight. After a while I realised that these people were drunk, and it was only ten in the morning. Our guide told us to wait while he went in search of the gatekeeper.

He returned fifteen minutes later to tell us that the gatekeeper was drinking in the bar. This was his day off and he wasn't taking anybody to any mountain. We were flummoxed. We had come all this way for nothing? We asked our guide to go back and explain to the gatekeeper that we had travelled from Johannesburg and we were not about to leave without some contact with the ancestors. Our gracious host did as we asked and after an hour and a half or so he returned with a forthright-looking woman who was high as a kite on, judging from her breath, brandy or whisky. We tried to communicate, knowing that there was no way we were going to get through as she stared back at us with her drunken, vacant eyes. Something must have penetrated, though, because she told us that if we brought our car up in another couple of hours and gave her and her husband a lift to their homestead, the gatekeeper would see us at midnight, after he had slept off the alcohol.

Naively, or more out of a feeling that we had absolutely no choice, we went back to the kraal to collect our car. Our host said that he would be our navigator and would then return home on foot once we had collected the gatekeeper and his wife.

It was dark by the time the intoxicated couple bundled themselves onto the back seat of our car. To me, it was an absolute miracle that they successfully directed us to their dwelling. There were many huts on very high ground. Strangely, even though it was in the same locality as the kraal we had stayed in the night before, even in the dark, one could see it was green and surrounded by trees and boasted a magnificent view.

When we looked up at the night sky, it was covered in stars; it literally sparkled with them. We napped in the car, having been told that we would be called when the gatekeeper was ready to see us.

At midnight, there was a gentle knock on the car window on the driver's side. Farai wound down the window and a young man with the most serene face I had ever seen peered in. He informed us that the gatekeeper was ready to see us.

We were led to a hut nestled on the side of a mountain. The young man waved us in and then stepped aside as we entered tentatively, adjusting to the candlelight inside.

The gatekeeper was sitting on the floor in the middle of the hut, his legs stretched out in front of him. He waved for us to sit down, a bottle of something placed neatly by his side. He then instructed us to pay him. We handed over the money. He counted it several times, then proceeded to tell us that this was not the season for talking to the mountain. He told us that we would have to come back later in the year. Something inside me snapped. I was sick of being shoved around, being taken for a ride again and again and again. In poverty, was there no honour, no pride, no honest to goodness . . . integrity? Why was everything a con—from human relationships to working relationships to spiritual relationships? I felt as if I was going to burst and I really didn't care that he didn't speak a word of English.

I basically demanded of the gatekeeper that he take us to the mountain, having made us wait for him all day while he drank himself into a stupor. He was aggressive and defensive and retaliated by saying that the amount of money we had brought was wrong, so even if it were the right season he would not have been able to take us with the cash we had given him. I couldn't believe it. I burst into tears and told him that he would be punished for dishonouring my ancestors.

I got up and left that hut as he worriedly asked Farai where I was going. There was a tree looking over the mountain's edge. I leant against it and begged my grandmother to step in and help me since I was following her instruction to talk to her through the mountain.

The feeling of betrayal that had become the norm for me at this time in my life threatened to consume me once again. With some effort I pulled myself together and made my way back into the hut.

The gatekeeper stubbornly stared at me. Farai explained that he was refusing to budge. There would be no going to the mountain, but he would keep the money because of the time he had given us and would be happy to read the bones for me. I told him I came to speak with my ancestors and I didn't need the bones to be thrown for me. What followed next remains in my memory as somewhat unearthly. It was like I was transported into some fantasy world that was unfamiliar yet familiar.

Suddenly, I saw three people glide—and I mean *glide*—into the hut. One was a beautiful, dark-skinned woman with short, silver hair, the second was the gatekeeper's wife—who seemed very sober—and the third was the young man who had led us to the hut earlier. They sat around me in a very protective fashion. The gate-keeper almost cowered. The woman with silver hair spoke very gently to me. She said that she was sorry for what had happened to me. She said that I had been wronged and that she had instructed the gatekeeper to return my money. She said that he was not fit to take me to the mountain and that I needed to return when the right person would take me. She never specified when that would be. The gatekeeper returned the money and the woman and the young man left as swiftly as they had arrived.

The gatekeeper's wife remained behind to apologise again and promise us that the gatekeeper would see us the next morning at five before we left for Johannesburg. We said goodnight and left the hut.

The young man was waiting for us outside, ready to escort us back to the car. On the way he told us that we had helped to expose a situation that had been brewing for quite some time.

The gatekeeper was a fraud, but they could not find proof of this so they could not oust him and put the correct gatekeeper in his place.

It was a very big moment in the history of the mountain because the present gatekeeper belonged to a line of fraudsters who had disobeyed the wishes of the ancestors. Apparently, the ancestors had specified that the mountain would not speak to any persons of European decent and that any individuals of this ethnicity were not to be allowed to hear the secrets of the mountain. If this law was broken, the mountain would stop communicating. Well, this present gatekeeper's line had broken the rule and the mountain had stopped talking. They had prayed for this gatekeeper to slip up so they could finally set the record straight. It would seem that they now had ammunition to take him to trial and remove him.

How we found ourselves in the middle of this power struggle is beyond me, but it would seem that we contributed to setting some part of this crazy history right.

At five am we were in the fake gatekeeper's hut once again. He was now dressed in ceremonial garb of some sort and made a show of throwing bones and doing a very superficial reading. We left. Finally.

I had no answers from the ancestors and felt even more at sea than ever. Back to Hellsville, to the saga of the Sapienses and Spike. I wished I was someone else.

13

It was as if that trip pushed Farai deeper into the abyss. I hardly ever saw him and when I did his eyes never quite focused on anything—the effects of cocaine, a drug that alters personality. Farai would go from being just plain vacant to being aggressive and generally unpleasant. He was leaving me more and more to deal with his family. His brother would literally order me to take him to get his medication. His mother was constantly moaning that I wouldn't buy her a house in Zimbabwe, as if I, for some reason, must make up for her ex-husband's neglect. Even the bathroom floor was no longer a place of comfort—there was no escape from the fires raging inside of me. I had no idea how to extinguish those flames.

The producers from *Zulu Love Letter* contacted me to inform me that I had been invited to Fespaco, the international film festival held in Ouagadougou, Burkina Faso. I saw another opportunity to get Farai away from Spike and into a place where he and I could seriously talk about our life. The producers informed me that the invitation was for me only, as they just did not have the funds to pay for Farai's ticket. As usual, I fought Farai's corner; as usual, he just sat back and watched me hammer another nail into my own coffin when I announced, with bravado, that if Farai, my husband, couldn't go, then neither would I.

The producers went all the same. I stayed rotting in the sick world I had worked so hard to create. My only experience of winning the best actress award at the 2005 Fespaco film festival was a phone call from one of the producers at midnight, congratulating me profusely on a job well done. A week later, he gave me the award in a café in Johannesburg.

Through all that transpired after that day, my award is the one item I still have, and it occupies a place of honour in my home.

This, thanks to my sister, Quezi, who once said I must never let that representation of my hard work out of my sight.

One other jewel, perhaps the last before everything was shot to hell, was given me in the form of an invitation from Zindzi Mandela to visit her home.

When I stepped into the kitchen of Zindzi's home, there was this beautiful, tall woman on crutches standing by the door. She had apparently sprained one of her ankles. I glanced up at her and made an utter fool of myself as my mouth flew open and incoherent sounds started tumbling out of it. I was looking up at Winnie Madikizela-Mandela.

She put a gentle hand on my shoulder and told me that she was so happy to meet me at last. I thought I was going to pass out! How could an ordinary human such as myself have the great fortune to meet both Nelson and Winnie Mandela in the space of only a few months? We spoke for some time about the state of the country and how the South African people were working to disentangle themselves from the injustices planted by apartheid. Imagine little old me having this very serious discussion with a freedom fighter, a leader, a soldier for equality.

Winnie then asked me what was going on in my industry. I told her of my experiences, explaining that things were not as they should be and that there was still a lot of work to be done. She responded with what I can only now view as an instruction. She said that when she saw me on the screen she felt that I would be "one of the ones" to make a difference.

I shrank inside at that moment because I had made such a mess of my life that I wasn't sure how to take her words. Such an extraordinary energy.

Winnie was nothing like the mad, out-of-control individual I had heard about. This woman was the epitome of sophistication. She was soft-spoken, intelligent and respectful. As a black woman, if she was angry, I was right there with her. I left Winnie Madikizela-Mandela that day knowing, once I had found my way back to daylight in my life, I would have to take up the baton and do my part.

Leaving cloud nine—Zindzi Mandela's house—I crashed-landed back in the hard, cold facts of my abnormal existence.

When I got home, my living room was full of people. Two of them were Farai and Spike. They were entertaining their friends in my house with seemingly no thought as to how I might feel about this. However, instead of walking in and telling these individuals to get the hell out of my house, for some reason I became the perfect hostess, trying to claim my territory, trying to send a message to Spike. I was drowning and Farai's strange Zimbabwean friends observed this scenario with keen interest. Eventually, I surrendered and told them I was going out. One of the guests, a young man (I am going to call him Slippery Joe because we will meet him later and he had an older brother who was so bad he doesn't even warrant a mention on the pages of this book), actually pointed out that it was my house and I should not have to leave my own house if I didn't want to.

I was speechless. It was as if he was speaking another language.

My brain could not interpret what he was saying; my level of self-respect had deteriorated to the point where I was now lying down in order to take the kicks. Spike and Farai were very busy floating around in la-la land, pretending that my house was their home and that they had every right to be there as a couple, entertaining their friends. Delusion. Scary stuff.

I ended up wandering around a mall. I saw a movie, treated myself to dinner and daydreamed about my meeting with Winnie Mandela. Wandering around so I didn't have to go home was becoming a regular part of my daily routine.

That night I received a call on my cellphone from New York. It was Quezi, my sister who had finally been released from South Africa at the age of five by order of the British government. She was coming over for a visit. I had not seen her for several years so I was delighted. Not only would it be great to see her, but it would give me the opportunity to meet my two nephews.

As you have probably gathered, I did not have a lot of interaction with my family during this period. My life was consumed by my toxic relationship and I was constantly pushing my family away. Quezi spent most of her time in Cape Town with my mother, but there was a point when I invited her to come and stay with me in Johannesburg. She accepted the invitation.

When people have had to deal with victims of abuse, they usually complain profusely about the fact that the victim is impossible to communicate with and that they inevitably return to their abusers and are therefore not worth the time and effort. A victim of abuse is exactly the same as someone experiencing a nervous breakdown. He or she is in hell, trapped by his or her own nightmare, and a great deal of compassion is required to help them heal and come out into the light.

It is not a question of them simply "pulling themselves together". It is an illness. They, like a person suffering from depression, are ill at ease.

I was ill at ease and somehow Quezi seemed to understand this because she did not focus on my surroundings. She focused on me. We talked and talked and talked.

The Puppeteer could not hide her irritation at my sister's presence. She could feel me waking up, because for once one of my tribe was around me. I was able to see where I came from, who I was, and therefore I was waking up to the fact that I had choices.

Easter weekend arrived and Farai's cousin persuaded me that it would be a good idea for us to go away together. She had a new beau and she had this picture in her head of us "couples" enjoying a weekend as a group. Slippery Joe's brother was also in the country with his wife. I shudder when I think of the people that surrounded me at that time, a true reflection of how I had grown to totally disrespect my life. I invited my sister to join us and, after much resistance, she agreed.

We drove out to the Magaliesberg, Credo Mutwa's country. We had booked several little bungalows with a communal swimming pool. All around us were the dramatic mountains, staring down at us, defiant in their majesty.

The first night was pretty uneventful, except that Farai made friends with the people in one of the bungalows nearby. They were people who Farai would not ordinarily mix with—a young biking couple—and when he introduced them to me they could barely open their mouths because they were so high from whatever cocktail of drugs they had been feasting on. It was then that I understood what had drawn Farai to them.

Farai had become a serious addict. The following day he started getting agitated and told me that he wanted to go back to Johannesburg. I begged him to just get through the next couple of days, but as the hours passed he became more and more erratic and by the time evening arrived he was spinning out of control. It was so bad that I decided to call for help. Unfortunately, we were deep in the valley, so getting a signal was nearly impossible. Suddenly Farai was in his cousin's car. Why the woman gave him the keys, considering the state he was in, is beyond me. He sped off and two seconds later we heard a loud crash. His cousin's beau and Slippery Joe's brother just stood there like a couple of zombies. I screamed for them to go and help Farai out as I continued to try and get a signal.

They took one of their cars and came back with Farai sitting in the back like a statue, his back as straight as a poker. I opened the door and asked him to please come out. Suddenly he sprang to life, roared like a lion and leapt across the seat towards me, screaming. I slammed the car door shut. He had lost his humanity; he was like this wild, rabid animal.

I decided to try calling from in front of one of the bungalows, hoping I could get a signal there, when I heard a loud cry. It was my sister's voice.

When I got to where the sound had come from, I found my sister lying on the floor. Farai's cousin's beau was just standing there, Slippery Joe's brother was just standing there, and Farai was climbing into a car with his junkie friends.

I ran to my sister. She told me that Farai had come out of nowhere, lifted her off the ground and bashed her against the wall. My sister is tiny. I asked her where all the men were at the time. She told me that they had been right there and that they had done nothing.

That night I decided that I would not be going back to Farai. The whole thing had to end or somebody was going to die.

The next morning Farai's cousin had to get someone to fix her car. Meanwhile, Slippery Joe's brother was out of there like a bat out of hell. I asked the cousin's beau if he would be a witness, as I had decided to lay charges against Farai for assaulting my sister. He refused. I did not feel like spending any more time around these people, but my sister and I were stranded in the middle of nowhere. I finally got a signal and called the only people I could count on—two beautiful women who ran a spa I frequented. They were the only people I knew who would come to my rescue.

There, right there, was my realty. This was how isolated I had become.

The two women came and picked us up and my sister and I ended up staying in a hotel.

When we were booked safely into the hotel, I called Farai, who was ranting and raving, ordering me to come home and leave my sister where she was. My house was full of his family, friends and lovers, and none of them, including him, was paying a penny towards the bond. I basically told him I needed my car and arranged to have him leave it at one of the malls in a very exclusive part of Johannesburg. I then told him to drop the keys with the hairdressers I used to frequent so I could collect them from there. It was like being in my own horror movie. I did not want to see him, to be honest—I was terrified of him—so I had to hide in a place where I could see him enter the shop and leave again. I wanted to avoid being jumped by him.

I got my car back and thank goodness because that car turned out to be my most loyal and trusted companion.

I now had to find a lawyer, which I did with the help of the two women from the spa.

Things just went from bad to worse. The lawyer's fees were extortionate, but I didn't feel I had any choice in the matter. Luckily for me, I had a few episodes left on *Muvhango*, so I could ask for an advance. Meanwhile, my sister made a desperate call to my mother and asked to borrow some money from her. This weird pattern I had fallen into—of haemorrhaging money—was accelerating. I was begging and borrowing from absolutely everyone, not knowing how or when I would be able to pay them back.

Eventually, I found a place to rent—this while paying lawyer's fees and many other expenses that I won't go into. I couldn't get out of this very negative pattern. I was deadlocked.

I used to go to court with my lawyer—which was often, now that we were building our case—in a haze.

I had attempted to go to the house to get some clothes I needed for work. I was so terrified that I went to the police and asked for their protection. When we got to the house and rang the bell, Farai refused to open the gate.

It is the most surreal thing to be banned from entering your own home. On top of this, he refused to give me my clothes.

Even the police were incredulous. They tried to reason with him and asked him to show some compassion as I needed the clothes for work. He told them that I should get a court order if I wanted to set foot in the house. The police said that unfortunately there was nothing they could do as Farai was my husband and consequently they were not allowed to force their way onto the property. Like a robot, Farai kept repeating that I had to get a court order. He then ordered the domestic worker to go into the house and bring out some black bin bags. When I asked what was in them, Farai boldly demanded that I return to the house after taking my sister's clothes to her—yes, that's what the bags contained. The gate was then partially opened and the bags were unceremoniously thrown into the street. How did this man imagine treating me like this would win me over?

As the police led me back to my car, I told Farai I would be back with a court order and divorce papers.

The only emotion I can remember at this point was hate. I absolutely hated Farai. To me, he was the devil incarnate—I could almost see the horns and forked tail. It felt as if his demonic family members and friends had taken over the house as he exercised his slimy rights.

My father's demand for a prenuptial played over and over in my head. It still does.

ONCE AN EXILE,
ALWAYS AN EXILE

1

The divorce papers were drawn up. Farai was served and a date was set for us to meet in court.

As the day approached, I became more and more despondent because I had begun to realise that the law was inclined to have a sympathetic ear for the male member in this kind of dispute. I will never forget sitting in the female judge's office after she had perused the document put together by my lawyer expressing my legitimate grounds for divorce—that of emotional abuse and the threat of physical abuse. It was clear that I had purchased the house and it was still in my name only. Despite this, the judge was adamant that the law of "community of property" still stood. I was free to return to the house, she said, but under no circumstances could Farai be prevented from living there too. My lawyer reminded her that he had already hit my sister and I was therefore vulnerable. She shrugged and said I could live in one part of the house and he in the other. The fact that he may prove to be violently aggressive towards me was . . . well . . . by the by.

I was overwhelmed, yet again, by a sense of helplessness. I kept asking myself why every step I took towards change, progressive change, in my opinion, was being blocked. I felt how I imagine a sane person forced into a straightjacket might feel. I thought I was going crazy. It was like being in a padded cell where I could see people through some kind of glass, but every time I opened my mouth to speak all they saw was my mouth opening and shutting like a fish. Instead of attempting to understand me by opening the door, they kept it closed and dismissed me.

When you are constantly told you are insane and misguided, you begin to believe it.

At this point my alcohol consumption, that had already been way beyond normal limits, was through the roof. I would polish off half a bottle of vodka daily before midday and would drink steadily all day and far into the early hours of the following day. I did this every day for two years.

This, of course, did not serve to strengthen my case with my lawyer and he started to pressure me to meet with Farai, as this is what he was demanding. He had not turned up to any of the court hearings, which seemed to make absolutely no difference because his refusal to grant me a divorce was being upheld. Eventually, I agreed to meet him. I thought that maybe if he looked into my eyes he would see that it was over, that there was absolutely nothing left, that my total lack of respect for him would be so obvious that after the meeting he wouldn't want anything to do with me.

I sat at the table in the lawyer's office, with his young assistant next to me, wishing I had never agreed to meet with Farai. He was already half an hour late, which, to be honest, was good for Farai (he was consistently two to three hours late for every meeting he ever went to).

When Farai finally arrived I immediately picked up the tell-tale signs of the effects of cocaine. He was hyperactive when he walked into the room.

As he sat down opposite me, I tried to pick up the cup of coffee the lawyer's assistant had made for me, but my hands started to shake violently. I could feel the sting of tears behind my eyes in response to the chilling realisation that my reaction was a clear indication of the fact that I was a victim of abuse—now that I didn't need to keep up appearances it was apparent just how his presence affected me. I was completely overpowered by this "little man". This is the extent to which I had handed over my power.

Farai talked incessantly, rocking back and forth in his seat, his eyes darting all over the place. He appeared to be totally out of control and I was reminded of his erratic behaviour on the night that had brought us to this point. I also had a flashback to the last visit we had made to Zimbabwe together. Farai's grandmother had passed away and he had asked Slippery Joe's brother and his wife to accompany us to Zimbabwe for the funeral. That trip was one of the darkest episodes of my life.

To begin with, we had to stay at Slippery Joe's brother's house for a couple of nights. I was miserable. I couldn't put my finger on it, but that was one of the unhappiest houses I have ever had the misfortune of spending time in.

We then drove deep into the Zimbabwean countryside until we arrived at the village compound where the funeral was being held. There were hundreds of people and Slippery Joe's brother's wife and I were swept away by the women and handed patterned material to wrap around our hips. We then had to help feed the guests who had come to pay their respects. Later that night, we joined the men and entered the main hut where Farai's aunt sat with other relatives. Farai seemed high. When we entered, he threw himself prostrate at his aunt's feet and lay there for what seemed hours. After that, I never really had contact with him till we left because I was ordered to remain with the women. It was a bizarre two days and for some reason it played itself out in my mind as Farai rocked backwards and forwards in his chair in the lawyer's office.

I was so grateful he was out of my life—for good, as far as I was concerned.

The lawyer proposed to Farai that he work with me to sell the house, the proceeds of which would be equally divided between us. In typical Farai fashion, he threw in another proposal just to stall things. This man was not going to let go of his main source of income that easily; he was not about to return to a regular life where he might have to work to pay his way without a fight. He suddenly announced that he would buy the house from me. I was stunned. I felt like saying to him that there was no audience he needed to impress and, actually, the best way for him to walk out ahead would be for him to take the money that was guaranteed him on sale of the house. Yet more money *morally* he wasn't entitled to, but, fortunately for him, *legally* he could grab it with both hands. What shook me the most was the realisation that, with or without cocaine, Farai had always behaved this way—he had bluffed his way through life. I had let him use my success, my wealth, my hard work to hustle his way into those arenas that made him feel important. That was all he wanted out of life and he had no intention of working for it. I was the perfect patsy. I wanted to throw up. The level of disgust I felt for myself is extremely hard to articulate—impossible, in fact. How was I to recover from this? How the hell was I going to regain any self-respect? I was crushed.

I feebly asked Farai what he was talking about in relation to buying my house. I pointed out to him that he had no money.

He almost leapt across the table, screaming that he had his own wealth, that actually he could get on fine without the "great Pamela Nomvete"—those were his words.

I simply repeated that he had no money.

This is where my lawyer also became my enemy. He told Farai that we would agree to his proposal. I couldn't believe it. I had explicitly told him that nothing Farai said could be counted on—he had not delivered on any of his promises up to this point.

When Farai left, I told the lawyer in no uncertain terms that he would never scrape together the money to buy my house and walked out of his offices in a daze.

I went to see my sister, my bottle of vodka in tow, and shared the events of this horrendous morning with her. The outcome was that she and I decided to put together a healing programme for victims of abuse.

2

My sister wrote two plays, one in which I shared my story of abuse and another which was a two-hander with an actress friend of mine who was deaf. This second play depicted two women who are unashamedly cruel and abusive to each other, the one being black and the other being white and deaf. We followed the plays up with discussions and workshops that ran over a couple of days. The impact on the communities we reached with this programme was overwhelming and truly gratifying. The fact that this well-known figure, who was seen as affluent and came from a stable background, was a victim of abuse encouraged people to speak out about their own situations.

Many of them vowed to take what they had learned from the programme and implement it in their own communities. My sister and I even won a humanitarian award for the work we did.

What of my career? My last role was on a television series called *Hard Copy*—a show about a newspaper. During this job I was continually shutting down and found it increasingly difficult to work. During one shoot a director spoke to me in such a disrespectful way that I did something I have never done before or since: I began to cry on set. Silent tears fell down my cheeks. I decided there and then that I couldn't educate young people about abuse and tell them how to change their own lives while I was functioning in a totally abusive environment.

I pretty much retired from acting and tried to throw myself into the programme I had created with my sister.

Money was tight, though thanks to the one organisation, Hope Worldwide, we managed to get funding for quite a few gigs. This, however, was not enough to pay bills and eat. My life was on the decline again. It was exhausting trying to get funding from institutions which claimed to be working towards bettering the lives of those in South Africa's poorest communities. Our programme seemed to be far too empowering and this was somehow threatening. Its overall message was to encourage people to take control of their lives and not be victims of any negative situations they found themselves in. This seemed to leave a bad taste in the mouths of these institutions. It was unbelievably frustrating, especially since we had proof that the programme worked.

The last thing we did, before my sister felt it was time for her to move on, was a small tour—with a budget of approximately nothing—that was yet another success. It was the strangest thing. I went to several colleagues, acquaintances and so on to ask for support. Their responses were consistent—all in the vein of them not being able to see the value of such a project and that the initiative did not, in their opinion, offer sustainability. What they meant was "monetary" value and "financial" sustainability. The fact that it was literally changing perceptions, empowering young people and bringing them to the realisation that treating one another with respect, as well as respecting themselves, was the way forward, had no value for those who had the means to support it.

That the young people in question were begging for this programme to come to their communities also made absolutely no difference to those who were able to ensure that it did.

My landlord visited me one fine Sunday morning and told me that I was behind on my rent and that they were asking me to leave. I defiantly agreed to move within three days. This meant frantically looking through newspapers, making calls and going to view properties. The places I could afford were on the whole uninhabitable. In the end, I accepted what seemed to be the best one. This was a modest dwelling with a bathroom, a bedroom, a living room and a loft that I later discovered was infested with rats. When I reported this to the landlady, she was nonchalant—simply confirming that there were many on the property. I hardly slept while living there because I was plagued by nightmares in which I was attacked by the rodents, who were now my housemates.

Things became so dire that I had to start selling some of my belongings. It was at this point that I learned the art of doing away with excess.

Do you realise that I had two cellphones? I believed that it was absolutely necessary to have them until the moment I worked out that the two things that would probably sell pretty quickly, and for a reasonable price, were one of my cellphones and my clothes.

I had still not been able to recover my clothes from Farai's clutches, but there were some in my possession that I felt I could get rid of. I began stopping people in the street in an attempt to sell what I had.

There were good days and bad days, in that I would sell three or four items one day and nothing the next. The irony was that the people I was selling to were even poorer than I was and they were also my fans. I could see the questions spilling out from behind their eyes as they examined my goods, wondering why Pamela Nomvete was walking around with various items of clothing, trying to sell them to the people she stopped in the street.

I found myself constantly demanding money from my family without really telling them what was happening to me. Being the good people they are, they would send me bits and pieces, thinking I was being irresponsible or maybe being influenced by my husband.

Eventually, I accumulated just enough to get out of the rat hutch and move into digs that were more comfortable. I even managed to get a voice-over job that allowed me to supplement what I had, and for the first time in months I was able to buy a bed. It felt so good to not sleep on a cold, hard floor. I realised how all my life I had taken sleeping in a bed for granted. At this moment, I realised it was in fact a luxury for many. I found I could also buy a fridge. It hardly had any food in it, but I bought it all the same.

Still, I could not bear the idea of going back and working in an industry that was, for me, the definition of exploitation and abuse, as well as a place where Farai could find me and continue his harassment. I was trapped.

I had basically gone into hiding but had no concept of this at the time. I was terrified that if I continued my career, and became visible, he would find me. I had given Farai power over my life, to the point of throwing away my house, my money, my career and my ability to live. I suffered from headaches all day long; my staple diet was coffee and cigarettes.

Then a very odd thing happened to me. Out of the blue, I was contacted by *Carte Blanche*. To be honest, I don't even remember what the theme of the show was. All I know is that I agreed to appear on it.

I told them that they would have to provide me with an outfit or give me the money to buy one. They agreed to provide it and, two days later, I was on a plane to Cape Town for a one-day shoot.

Arriving on that set was like returning to a ghostly version of my past life. A young actress called Chichi Letswalo introduced herself to me and I found myself full of admiration for her dynamic young energy. I told her about the healing programme my sister and I had created and how we were unable to continue because of a lack of support. She listened earnestly and expressed deep regret that this programme was not still in existence. *Carte Blanche* put us up in a hotel for the night, as shooting finished late—we were booked on a flight back to Johannesburg early the next morning. Chichi and I sat up talking until about midnight, sharing our experiences of being artists in South Africa and talking about the challenges that we all faced. We so wanted to do the right thing.

On hearing more about how my sister and I had poured our own resources into the healing project, Chichi concluded we needed "supernatural intervention". I remember staring at her and thinking that she was right because I kept feeling that we needed a miracle, so I guessed "supernatural intervention" amounted to the same thing. She suggested I meet her pastor, who she described as a very spiritual and insightful man. I agreed and thus began the next leg of my journey into the world of spirit.

3

I met Brother Brown in the church building—technically a warehouse—in downtown Johannesburg. The name of the church I cannot disclose, but suffice it to say that it had the word *Christ* in it.

I tried to keep an open mind as I observed the various groups of people scattered around the vast open space. From time to time I would hear loud cries of "Praise the Lord!" and "Thank you, Jesus!" as Chichi led me to a seated area. Within minutes a young, trendy Nigerian man approached us. Chichi made the introductions and he immediately acknowledged who I was, expressing his pleasure at meeting me. We sat down and I told him the challenges I was facing and the clarity I needed to continue the programme. He listened intensely and then began to tell me that my talent was such that he could see my success reaching unimaginable heights. He saw me working in all kinds of arenas with all kinds of people, but he felt that the only way I would be able to achieve all of this was if I gave myself to Christ.

I told him I would.

Chichi nearly fell off her chair in shock as I nodded and repeated that I would. I said to them that if this was God's will, then so be it, because I had run out of ideas.

Brother Brown suggested that I return the following evening because there was going to be all-night prayer meeting that would end at five am. I told him I would be there.

Does any of this seem familiar to you? Put it this way, leaving the warehouse church I felt the same way as I had when leaving Credo Mutwa or the sangoma in Soweto. It was curious to me that Credo and the Soweto brother had told me to dance to the beat of the drum and go and converse with the ancestors if I were to find any peace in my life.

Now here was this "man of God" telling me that if I was to find any peace I needed to give myself to Christ, to obey and follow God's law.

My conclusion is that all these great seers were advising me to find my spiritual voice in order to get the right perspective on my life. It's just that they all believed their way was the true way.

I did go for that all-night prayer meeting and experienced something I had never experienced before. The last time I had attended a church service I had observed people singing hymns, the preacher giving his interpretation of the messages in the Bible and a congregation kneeling or bowing their heads in prayer. My experience of the warehouse church was dynamic, to say the least. People speaking in "tongues" were touched by the Holy Spirit, which meant they would go flying in all directions, taking chairs and people with them. I was intrigued. While I didn't speak in tongues, I did pray and left at four am. Brother Brown was impressed and told me that I was one of God's chosen because I obviously meant business. I needed answers, I needed a great deal of help and where better to get it than from the "creator of all things"?

I contacted a lawyer in Pretoria, a man from Botswana who had helped me once before. I told him that I was trying to get a divorce from Farai but he was not willing to let go of the marriage. This lawyer agreed to help me, even though he knew both of us. I felt this factor may serve me well as Farai might be more inclined to follow the advice of someone he knew. I even went to an estate agent and said I wanted to sell the house. I explained my absurd situation and one of the agents, despite this, agreed to try to sell the house.

A middle-aged woman, who I will call Molly, came with me to view the house a few days later (after I had gone through the gruelling exercise of getting the lawyer to tell Farai I was entitled to open up the option of selling to other buyers, in case he was unable to meet the asking price). He had not come back with an offer, of course, but continued to claim that he would.

I have a feeling that he must have entered into some stupid dialogue with Slippery Joe's brother and they had conned each other into believing that they were going to buy the house from me.

The first shock—on our arrival—was Slippery Joe coming to the gate when we rang the bell and telling us that we weren't allowed in because Farai wasn't home. I reminded the little twerp that the house was mine and that Farai had agreed to allow the estate agent to view it. Still, the stranger on my land refused to open the gate. I called over the police detail I had asked to accompany us, something I did every time I visited that house. As soon as Slippery Joe saw the uniformed gentleman he was quick to open the gate.

When I entered the house, I was shocked at what I found. The house had once been beautiful. It had a great deal of space and serious style. The living room seemed dark, lifeless. In one corner were two blown-up photographs of me from a shoot that I had done some time previously. It was surreal, almost as if Farai was keeping the photographs to prick his conscious while he filled the house with people I definitely would not have approved of.

What was once the study now had a bed in it and the television room was a bedroom too.

I had seen enough and told the estate agent that I would wait for her outside. I waited on the other side of the gate, off the grounds of what was no longer my home. I wanted no part of it. I was well aware that my clothes were still sitting in the wardrobes upstairs, but I was happy to let them go.

The policeman, I noticed, then asked for Slippery Joe's papers. I saw fear well up in his eyes, but he produced documents that seemed acceptable to him.

After checking Slippery Joe's papers, the policeman went into the house. He emerged a few minutes later with Farai's brother and told me that he was an illegal immigrant and that he would be taking him away to be deported. I have to say I was thrilled to hear this. All my feelings of "there should be no borders between African countries" momentarily vanished. I felt the sweet sensation of revenge wash over me—*yes, throw that bastard out of my house, even better, out of the country.*

Molly pointed out that there was rising damp in one corner of the house that would affect the price, but not drastically if we managed to sell fairly swiftly.

In two to three weeks she'd had three or four offers, having fought incessantly with Farai to get prospective buyers into the house. She described how Farai would make the arrangements to allow her in and then simply just not be there when she turned up. One of the offers was cash and for pretty much the asking price. It fell through because Farai refused to sign the documents giving his consent for the sale.

Molly stayed in the fight for about three or four months, even though the value of the house had dropped drastically by the end of this period because the rising damp had by then spread dramatically. The damp made me realise that one's surroundings can, absolutely, reflect the state of one's life. The energy in that house was one of decay and that was now being reflected in its walls.

Eventually, the estate agent and I parted ways and I went to my bank, informing them that I would not be paying the next instalment on my bond so they may as well repossess the house. They informed me that the procedure was to wait three months before they took such action.

They completely ignored the fact that I was informing them in advance that I would not be paying. Farai's luck was in because the bank had no imagination beyond the terms as set out in the agreement. For three more months he and his posse would enjoy the house.

Once the three months were up, the bank slammed a repossession order on the house, putting it up for auction, and Farai finally woke up to the fact that the house was not going to draw me back into his life.

I received a phone call one morning from a woman who said she had seen the house was going up for auction and had put in an offer to buy, which Farai had agreed to. We had to get everything signed off and in the courts by lunchtime the following day. Between this woman, her husband and me, we managed to complete all the paperwork literally five minutes before the auction was closed.

When it was done, I looked at the situation, recognising, once again, that this was an example of what my relationship with Farai was about.

I was the one doing the running around, trying to make things happen, while he looked on and reaped all the benefits.

Two weeks after the sale, I was called by the new owners. They said that I was welcome to come and collect the items that Farai had left behind. They were most apologetic when they informed me that he had taken almost every single thing in the house, from the furniture to the paintings on the walls. The only things left were my clothes, my passport in the safe and the two blown-up photographs of me, because the buyers would not let him take them. As I walked into the empty living room, it hit me. This man was a thief, pure and simple. He and his brother, the Artful Dodger, were a team. This was his job, which was why he wasn't able to hold down a regular job. Amazing! I had opened my home for years to a professional, small-time thief. Incredible! How humiliating! In that moment, I did not trust myself at all. I felt like a total loser. So stupid.

I had turned up at the house with a roll of black bags for my clothes. As I was piling the now full bags into my car, I noticed a woman watching me from the house. I walked up to her and asked if she worked there. She told me that she did and asked for my autograph to take to her daughter. I asked if she liked the photographs and when she said she absolutely did I walked into the house and gave them to her with my blessing.

The gratitude with which she received them humbled me beyond words and remains the highlight of my life as a "celebrity". Following a suggestion from my sister, I drove straight to a church and offered the clothes for charity. I was further humbled by the reception I was given. I was told that there had been a flood in the northern part of the country and people there were desperate for clothes.

What they didn't realise was the gratitude was all mine; they were helping me move on from my unwanted past.

Even after all this—the house being gone, the public appearances being gone, the money being gone—Farai still refused to sign the divorce papers.

The lawyer took the money from the sale of the house and put it in a trust until such time as the divorce was finalised. This meant, of course, that the longer the divorce proceedings dragged on, the more money would go on legal fees. I guess Farai had been so used to spending another person's money that he had no idea that money can run out. He obviously thought I was still working and would be supporting him for the rest of his life. No one explained to him that the life-support machine had been turned off.

4

The pressure was mounting. My financial situation was deteriorating rapidly. My sense of "self" had long faded and I was being consumed by negative elements in my makeup that were driving me to believe I was a useless member of society, a "waste of space". The only thing that offered a glimmer of hope was my relationship with God. Church and all the things it promised was the only thing that made me get up in the morning.

I was smoking constantly; a cigarette brought me a great deal of comfort. Nicotine is the most available drug on the market. The one thing I could not do without: cigarettes. On the days my purse was completely empty, I would walk along the streets, searching for stubs on the ground, desperate for even a secondary hit of nicotine. I developed a friendship with one of the attendants at the local petrol station who would sell me loose cigarettes.

The two things that had me scrambling around for change or desperately trying to sell more items of clothing were the need for cigarettes and collection at the warehouse church. I was an educated woman, I had seen the world, and I had parents with wonderful values who had provided a stable home environment. Yet now, having to manage my own life, I was failing miserably.

I was soaking up all the sermons given by the swanky priests with their well-educated Nigerian accents in the warehouse church. I recognised them because I had grown up with people like them.

I remember bursting into laughter at one of the sermons when the priest said: "They will tell you it's not about the money, but I am here to tell you it is. It's all about the money." He then proceeded to encourage us to dig deep into our pockets and give to God because that act of giving would mean we would be rewarded ten times over.

There were days when I had only twenty rand to my name, and I needed that money to put petrol in my car, but I would give up that twenty at a service at the warehouse church, then wonder how the hell I was going to drive back home without petrol. On many occasions, I simply asked members of the congregation for petrol money. Many refused me, but many convinced themselves I was a charity case and that God would reward them handsomely for helping me out.

I remember deciding that I needed to learn how to speak in tongues—at the time I had this strong sense that if I could utter the right prayers, the ones that reached God's ears directly, my situation would change. I prayed constantly for a miracle. I prayed for money to somehow manifest in my bank account. I prayed to have God appear to me like He had to Moses and all the saints. I prayed to hear God's voice whispering directly in my ear because I had heard that it had happened to so many. I was willing myself to believe and it worked.

One of the things I was constantly forgetting, or perhaps wishing away, was my fame. Everyone in the church recognised me and it was even worse when Chichi and I were together. So more and more people began to hang around us. They wanted to pray with us all the time. It was therefore easy for me to go to one of the senior members in the church and request a crash course on praying in tongues. She took me to one side and explained in earnest that the language of "speaking in tongues" was just that: a language. She told me that it was the language of heaven and because of this you didn't actually learn it. Instead, God would grace you with the ability to speak, if you opened your heart fully to him. I was pretty desperate, so I could not imagine God would fail to grace me with this ability, if I just trusted Him and went for it.

She placed her hand on my head and ordered me to speak. I couldn't, I didn't know how, but she just kept right on yelling for me to speak. So I did.

People around me began staring at me in awe. They commented that they could feel the heat from heaven emanating from my body.

What they felt was my desperate need for answers, my longing to find clarity. I needed an answer from God, I needed Him to respond to my cry for help, for redemption from this terrible horror movie that was my life. I needed to be free from my own nightmares. I wanted out.

Nothing happened. I didn't hear God's voice in my ear. There was no miracle.

The woman told me that I had courage and strong faith and that was all God needed from me. Then she wished me goodnight.

Two women who had witnessed this little spectacle came over to me. I will call them the Conniving Twins, as they were inseparable, even though they were not related. They always seemed to stand to one side and watch each member of the congregation, deciding who they were and where they put them on their private list of who was worthy of Christ's love and who wasn't. I, automatically, was one of the people at the top of their list because I was famous and they were determined to be seen rubbing shoulders with people like me. I met them because they had found their way into my friend Chichi's pocket. Now they rushed over to me and insisted God would reward me because He would surely recognise my strong faith. They said I would definitely be top of the list for bringing believers to the church and that I should immediately start my recruiting campaign so I could gain a prominent position in the church.

I was terribly confused. I was on the one hand flattered and reeling with the idea that perhaps I had some use in the world—could I be a church leader and bring God's lost sheep home? On the other I was horrified that there was some kind of weird competition going on and that somehow numbers being brought into the church would assure one's entry into heaven. Didn't heaven belong to everybody? This felt like a continuation of the insane career I was trying to leave behind, this idea that there were the "chosen" ones who made it and that being famous meant that some special light shone over you. Some-how, it all felt really wrong.

The twins insisted they needed to come to my house and pray with me or to meet up and watch DVDs of leading Christian preachers for inspiration. I ended up visiting the home of one of them, to watch a DVD, since I had no furniture in my house save my double bed and my fridge. When I think back to that time, it plays in my head like a frightening, out-of-control B-movie. There are elements of it that should have been all right, valuable in fact, but because the agendas were all wrong, it was a terrible and destructive mess.

The first time we met, we watched a DVD. Then, having been moved by the dramatic message of the dynamic preachers, which rang so true as we sat armed with our Bibles, following each chapter and verse referred to, we jumped up, held hands tightly and prayed with every fibre of our being, in tongues, to God. What happened on these occasions was that someone would be particularly taken over by the "spirit" and God would use him or her to speak through. It was potent stuff and I quickly realised that I had a gift for prophesying. I was able to tune into people, vibrations, energy, spirit, whatever you choose to call it, and would be able to tell them about their lives. I could see into their lives. It was crazy.

I kept asking myself, every time I did this, why I wasn't able to see into my own life and make the correct decisions for me. I wondered why God allowed me to help others with my "gift", yet He wouldn't allow me to use it to solve my own problems. That was one of the major problems I had with God. He didn't seem interested in my life unless I was suffering. He loved me, supposedly, but I wasn't good enough to be happy. I thought Christ had done all the suffering necessary for all of us, otherwise Him hanging off that cross in terrible pain and agony was surely all in vain. Where was our happiness in all of this? I guessed if He was willing to allow His only begotten son to endure that kind of torture, then who the hell was I to demand more? Oh, I wrestled with God daily. I railed at Him, fist in the air, as my circumstances deteriorated day by day, hour by hour. It seemed that as far as God was concerned, life was a punishment.

Now I think of it, everything that happened in this space with the Conniving Twins bore a remarkable resemblance to elements of African spirituality. When speaking to ancestors in African rituals, people go into fits, speak with the voice of the deceased and give guidance. So, in a way, it wasn't in strange that we were all comfortable with this form of worship, because it was a part of our heritage. However, we were doing it in the name of a religion that condemned all of this as unholy. I didn't think of it then, but now I am deeply concerned about my identity as an African.

There were times when one of the twins, the most vocal of the two, would spit at us while praying, in order to display the wrath of God. There was one time when the milder of the two had us praying in tongues in her home and at some high point she called out her seven-year-old son to pray with us. There was something really unnerving about seeing a young child vibrate with "the spirit".

As I watched, he broke the circle and came to me and started to pray over me. I fell to my knees and cried and cried. He told me that he loved me and wished me peace and love as I was one of God's agents. Everyone fell about in awe.

Afterwards, his mother told me that she had never heard him speak this way to anyone and that I was therefore to take his words seriously and ask God in earnest what He wanted me to do.

That night, when I got home, my electricity had been cut off. This was the height of winter in Johannesburg. I walked into the house, tried the lights, and, when they failed, my heart sank to the floor. My only comment was, "Here we go."

I struggled to find candles and succeeded, but it was just too cold and too dark for me to read my Bible. I went back into the garage and sat in the car. I warmed it up a bit and put on one of the CDs I had purchased—the preachings of an extremely powerful American pastor. I tell you those American evangelicals could convert a cardboard box. They are amazing. When you are literally living in the dark and the cold, as I was, when you are in hell in the physical world, they could lift you out of your reality. If they told you that if you just believed in the blood of Christ there was absolutely nothing to fear, then you would believe. If they told you that if you turned to God the father, the one who was here "before the beginning began, world without end," then *all* your troubles would vanish, then you would turn to God the father. I sat for hours, following the passages the preacher referred to, until I couldn't keep my eyes open.

The next morning, my landlady paid me a visit. Her message was short and sweet. If I did not come up with the rent in two weeks, she was going to have me thrown out. After that visit, I stupidly looked at the fridge, the only piece of furniture in the living/dining area, and then I went to the bedroom to check out the double bed. I left the house and was on my way to the petrol station, in search of the attendant who used to sell me loose cigarettes, when I realised that even if I sold my "furniture" I would not be able to pay the rent.

The petrol attendant was such a great guy. I will call him Joseph. He would encourage me every time I went to see him. He would tell me to hang in there. He was utterly perplexed that someone as successful as I was could be in the horrendous predicament in which I found myself. He kept saying that I needed to go to my friends in the television industry and ask for their help. I explained that they were now tired of me, that when you are a member of their club you are under the protection of that club, but when you leave, those doors close and stay very tightly shut, especially if you end up penniless. I was so ashamed of my circumstances. It took every bit of my will power to stand in front of a fan and beg him for free cigarettes, but he never made me feel bad. He just let me know that he would try to help me any which way he could. This was a man who could barely scrape enough money together to feed himself, let alone his wife and child.

Having left my friend, I returned to the house and began praying frantically in tongues, begging God to pull me out of the fires of hell.

I cried, sweated and threw myself on the floor, certain I must be reaching Him, when suddenly I had this urge to go the SABC and pray in its corridors, spread the blood of Christ along its contaminated walls. I sent a text message to the twins, as this was the only form of communication left to me. It was almost as if when I called, they would drop everything and come rushing to my side, like I was some kind of high priestess. I told them what God had instructed me to do. In half an hour we were at the reception of the SABC. I don't know how I managed to get the security and the receptionists to let me in with two women they had never seen before, but I did. This was further confirmation to all three of us that God had this whole thing under control and we were fulfilling His mission.

We walked quietly along the SABC's corridors and prayed. Bizarrely, it never occurred to me when performing this seemingly insane ritual that perhaps I should rather be asking if there was any work available for one of the so-called "top actresses" in the country. We walked along the studio floors, touching the walls and doors while praying earnestly under our breath in tongues, asking God to purify this condemned building and the people in it.

When we finished, the ladies took me for lunch and proceeded to hand me an envelope with money in it. I cried buckets because I needed that money: I needed to buy vodka, I needed cigarettes, I needed petrol in my car so I could go to church and do God's work, I needed to put something in the collection basket that Sunday and I needed to save so that I could pay my rent.

They both praised me, saying God had instructed them to give me this money. It all felt so right, but this was in fact the beginning of yet another unholy alliance that could have destroyed my life forever.

5

I received a text, as if the industry somehow knew I needed one last opportunity to humiliate myself. The text invited me to a celebration of the film *Tsotsi*—it had just won the Oscar for best foreign film. I nearly threw up on the invitation. It was amazing to me that South Africans had adopted a film that did not represent the true nature of the people of Soweto just because Hollywood had given it its stamp of approval. I wondered when we were going to stand up for ourselves as actors, as storytellers. The self-deprecating nature of the country seemed to reflect the self-loathing I had developed in my own life.

The gift from the Conniving Twins meant that I could down half a bottle of vodka, put petrol in my car and drive to what I considered to be a hateful event. They called it a celebration. I felt as if I were going to a funeral.

I walked into the tacky building where the event was being held. It was strange—an odd, office-type structure with crisps and so forth as snacks. The other thing that incensed me was that there was a picture of me in *Zulu Love Letter* so that those who had organised the event could boast about the films they had "supported". Remember the debacle in Venice?

What was even worse was that Forbidden Lover was now running the show. You can imagine the monsters that were rampaging through my head. I felt violated in every single way possible—all the sludge within was being reflected without, in Technicolor.

When I saw Forbidden Lover, I staggered up to him and told him that he had sold out. The arena was wrong and my timing was off. I may as well have put a loaded gun to my head and blown my brains out centre stage. The people at that gathering were all the usual suspects in the industry. That would be the last time I would ever see them and the last time they would ever see me.

When I got home to my cold, dark house, I threw myself on the floor and spewed out all the hateful words I could think of as a way of describing my life. That tenuous string in one's brain that holds everything together, that is the difference between making sense and falling apart, the difference between order and anarchy, had finally snapped.

Anarchy is, as we know, one of the ways to find lucidity. The nature of that lucidity is what can be most surprising, depending on how much you feel you have to lose. When you feel there is nothing to lose, it is amazing where the mind will take you.

A part of me felt like I had died.

I started a daily routine of jumping into a freezing shower and praying earnestly in tongues. I continued as I got dressed and went into the living room. I stopped only to have my morning cigarette: my comforter, my friend, my nourishment.

My cigarette finished, I went back and screamed at God and the heavens to give me answers as to how I was going to proceed with my life.

For an answer, I received an invitation to meet with one of the top executives at the SABC. I saw this as one thing and one thing only—an opportunity to deliver a message to her and to the organisation that she worked for from God. I had on previous occasions tried to reach this woman to pitch various ideas to her and had never been successful. After this very clear message "from God", I made one call, got through and was told to come and see her the following day. Imagine what that did for my faith! This God must be real. I had no idea of the nature of His message, but I knew He would guide me once I got to see this woman.

I informed the Conniving Twins of what I had been instructed to do. They told me they would be praying earnestly in support of my actions. I then scrambled around for change, hoping I could get a bread roll for breakfast. I lived in an empty one-bedroom house without electricity and therefore without hot water, was driving a Mercedes that had hardly any petrol in it and I didn't have two cents to rub together. It blew my mind to go into the supermarkets and see the majority of the population trying to feed their families. Sometimes I would stand in a corner and just watch how unjust life was. Food, one of man's most basic needs, was so expensive. Once they had purchased just enough for the family's evening meal, probably the only meal that household would get that day, they would have to make sure that there was enough change left over to get home. Moments like these made me grateful to be in the predicament I was in, otherwise I may never have really known how the majority of people in the country actually live.

I got home in one piece, having managed to get a roll and a sausage and a new supply of cigarettes. The food I had to pay for; the cigarettes I got for free.

As I prepared to feast, I saw there was a missed call from the lawyers on my phone. I sent them a "Please call me" request, something I had to do a lot at that point in my life. Within minutes, my phone rang. On hearing what the lawyer had to tell me, my knees went weak and could no longer hold me up. I sank to the floor with utter relief and a sense of accomplishment—Farai had finally agreed to sign the divorce papers. He had in fact done so, and the lawyer was requesting my presence in his offices so that I could sign my part of the agreement.

Once off the phone, thanks to the twins, I had some petrol in the car to get me to Pretoria to sign those papers. Again, I felt God was responding to me at last. I knew that there wouldn't be much money as Farai had held out for so long, but I would at least be able to pay my arrears on the rent and possibly have some money to live on till things turned around. Since I was already on my knees, I pressed my hands together and gave a small prayer of thanks.

When I returned from Pretoria later that afternoon, I was comforted by the fact that a court date had been set so that the law of the land could declare me a free woman. I was also relieved that the funds were to be released as soon as possible and I could get some breathing space regarding the roof over my head. That night, for the first time in a long time, I slept with the feeling that there was hope after all.

The following morning, taking that cold shower wasn't so bad.

That day was the day I was going to give thanks to the Lord by carrying out His command. Armed with a Bible, I entered the SABC building with purpose.

After signing in, I got into a lift and took it to some floor very near the sky.

When I walked into the office, a charming young woman greeted me and offered coffee.

The boss lady came out to lead me into her office a few minutes later and the coffee and biscuits were brought in as we settled on the couch.

After greeting each other warmly I swiftly got down to the business at hand. I told the lady that I had come to see her after being told by a higher authority to do so. She asked me who this higher authority was, expecting me to mention her bosses, I think, but I know she did not expect me to say "God".

I told her that I was there in front of her under instruction from God, the Creator. I believe what stopped her from throwing me out of her office immediately, aided by SABC security, was the conviction with which I spoke. In my mind, there was absolutely no doubt about what I was saying. I had told God that morning that I, because of my absolute faith, was willing to be a fool for Him. I was willing to be ridiculed, even persecuted, for bringing word of His will to humanity. All I wanted was to be His agent.

Before I gave the high-powered executive sitting in front of me the message from the Almighty, my prophesying skills kicked in and I was able to describe to her various dynamics in her household that I could have no prior knowledge of. It was almost as if I was being led to tell her these things to prove my legitimacy, so that she would be able to receive the actual message or warning that God had sent me to deliver.

It went something like this . . .

God was hugely disappointed with the way SABC was being run. He held them accountable for the negative images that were being transmitted to the young people of South Africa. He therefore was now taking matters into His own hands and had sent me to warn her of what was to come. She could either be responsible with her life or ignore Him and face the consequences. He declared that He was going to dismantle the SABC as we knew it and all those who were corrupt would be identified.

He declared that jobs and lives would be lost as a result of His wrath and there would be no one left standing, as He would not allow things to continue as they were. He would do this to get the SABC's attention, so that it could correct things, as this was the one institution in the entertainment world that was meant to represent the people and it had reneged on that promise: God had had enough. Her instruction was to fix things and create a new incorrupt structure that could turn into something the South African youth could feed on, so that they could grow to be champions.

By the time I had finished delivering God's word, this woman was on her knees, arms in the air, praising God and asking His forgiveness.

I stood, found a passage in my Bible and, with one hand held over her head, read it out loud. Then I left the room.

It was extraordinary. I felt that I had done my job and was ready for the next one. It was like someone else had taken over my body and I was okay with it.

Later that day I got a call from the executive, telling me that she knew I was an agent of God because when I stepped out of her office she had found a feather on her desk, a small white feather. It was impossible that it had come from elsewhere as all her windows were closed and, anyway, she was on something like the sixteenth floor.

There must have been a logical explanation, but it was an extraordinary thing to have happened. Someone—Dad, maybe—was definitely watching over me.

You know, for a moment, I understood how an assassin must operate. There was absolutely no emotional attachment to what I had done and what I was continuing to do.

I was ready for whatever hit list God had prepared for me, and I was going to honour that contract, no matter what. I had completed the first assignment and was raring to go.

Like I said earlier, I had nothing to lose. There was no turning back now.

6

I targeted several individuals who were presented to me by God and delivered messages accordingly. One was a man who wanted to leave his wife. I prayed over this man and told him from God's mouth to "be a man" and take responsibility for his family. There was a young woman, I now remember, who was suffering as a result of her husband being an alcoholic and was feeling defeated and alone. After praying for her, she said she felt empowered and was not going to allow herself to be a victim any more. It was extraordinary. My faith was at full throttle and I saw no barriers to completing the tasks God had set for me.

The more aggressive of the twins saw a wonderful opportunity here. It was, I suppose for her, going in for the kill, not unlike a dog when it smells the blood of a hare during a hunt. She knew all reason had left me, that I had no way to tell what was appropriate. I had been sucked into the God vortex and my life and all that it stood for was dead and buried. I was committing suicide slowly, trying to kill off my spirit and my soul.

The aggressive twin pulled me aside after a church service and said she needed to talk to me urgently. We sat in my car, which seemed to be the safest place for her to make her request—even the other twin was not to be let in on this one, or so she had me believe.

Once settled in the car, the aggressive twin began to tremble and kept burying her face in her hands. She told me how she had been in love with a certain gentleman for some time and God had told her that she was his wife. She went on to say that she needed another strong soldier of God to help her talk to this man and inform him of God's instruction that she was to be his wife and would lead him to his salvation. We then prayed and agreed to meet that night at the other twin's house to ask God for guidance on how we were to proceed.

This woman had recognised that I had lost touch with reality but the inherent qualities of my nature, that of courage and faith, were still intact. And because I now lacked wisdom, the ability to be discerning, she was going to manipulate me and what she saw as my "powers" to get what she wanted. It is so true that if you wish to know where you are at, just look at your environment. In terms of the company you keep, you will see your state of mind. We were all broken, desperate and lost, and we clung to the one thing that could accommodate us, because we couldn't see it, hear it, touch it or reason with it. In a word, it was as abstract as our lives had become. It was called God.

That night, we stood in a circle, holding hands and praying in tongues till we steered one another into frenzy. When I look back, I can now totally understand plays like *The Crucible*. It is so easy to work oneself up into a state of being that is totally out of control and intoxicated without the presence of drugs or alcohol. If one is susceptible to letting go and allowing the delusions of the mind to begin to take hold, there is no telling what one is capable of doing. There are these inherent elements in our makeup as human entities that, when exploited, can take one to the edge and over, if they are not balanced with those elements that anchor a person. There is such a thin line between a Ted Bundy, the serial killer, and a Beethoven, the creative genius.

Having reached our intoxicated state, God began to speak through me. The instruction was that we were to go to the man in question's house after seven days—the following Sunday. There we would pray for him and present the aggressive twin to him as his future wife. My instruction was to deliver her to this man and leave her with him.

This was another example of how the environment in which I found myself created extreme behaviour in women, especially young women, behaviour that I had never seen in any other society I had lived in. There was this sense of utter desperation—if one did not *hook* a man who was moneyed and successful, a woman could not go on living. Men in the new South Africa were hunted, especially the rising black, middle-class male. We were living the law of the jungle: the females were on heat and they were not at all interested in waiting to be noticed by the man they had set their sights on. The name of this game was to choose your target, snare him and conquer him. The problem was, once you got him, you had to fight off all the other marauding females who may have had him in their sights. I saw these women everywhere in Johannesburg, and here in the church, with its Ten Commandments and high moral demands, they were even more active.

And this is probably why the man we were hunting—on behalf of the aggressive twin—took what happened next in his stride. He was used to it. The only difference here was that a well-known actress was in the middle of the mess.

The aggressive twin suggested that she move in with me for the period prior to the "delivery date". Stupidly, I agreed. To be honest, it was unbearable having her around constantly. The only relief came from the fact that she had to go to work every day.

The price of nursing someone who was clearly unstable, over-bearing and extremely manipulative was a very high one. She was becoming more and more aggressive and out of control when we prayed. I started to pray at different times to her, which infuriated her and created an overwhelmingly toxic atmosphere. It was like being back in my house with Farai's family. My world just kept getting darker.

Day seven arrived. Full of the power and will of the Lord, we went to the gentleman's house to confront him.

Much to our utter dismay, he wasn't home. The aggressive twin insisted we wait. For her, this was it. She was here and she was going to follow through, no matter what.

We waited and we waited and we waited.

Finally, at about midnight she got out of the car, insisting I follow and knock on the front door again. We rang the bell and knocked repeatedly. Suddenly, we heard a faint noise from a part of the house that appeared to be in darkness. We called out and eventually a man came to the window. He told us that he was the housekeeper and that his boss was out. We insisted we had a very important message for the boss and we needed to see him. We asked if he would be so kind as to let us wait for him inside. After some *umming* and *ahhhing*, he came and opened the front door for us.

As we entered the house, the aggressive twin turned to me and uttered the phrase we often used as fundamental Christian evangelists: "Who is God? Who is God? In Him we trust."

The poor, unsuspecting employee had no idea how—by simply opening the front door—he had fed the faith of the two delusional individuals who were now in his employer's house. He was so gracious and sweet when he recognised who I was. He made us tea and coffee and sat with us.

We talked and waited.

It was approaching two am when the front door opened. Our hearts leapt into our mouths as we prepared to come face to face with our purpose for being there.

A young woman and two young men walked into the living room. They were all very high on something—I am not quite sure what, but it was definitely stronger than just alcohol. We greeted them and introduced ourselves. They responded with the usual expressions of delight and familiarity on recognising the "television star". They asked where I had been hiding and when I was coming back to the screen. I remember there being a lot of tension in the air, emanating, primarily, from the young woman, but I cannot for the life of me remember what started it. Eventually, the three of them left and the twin and I were alone once more with the gracious employee. It was now daylight, around ten am, and I had had enough. I wanted to leave.

The twin lost it when I expressed my desire to leave. She would not hear of it; she ranted and raved and told me in no uncertain terms that she was not leaving because this was her husband and her house. In response, I suggested that she stay and claim her place next to her husband and I would go home, having completed God's work in delivering her to her man.

As her luck would have it, her delaying tactics worked. The man in question walked in with two women. One was introduced to me as his eldest sister. I cannot tell you who the other woman was, although I concluded at the time that she was another one of his conquests. He told us that he had received a call from his brother—obviously one of the two men we had met earlier—telling him of our continued presence in his house and had come to sort things out. He had, he continued, brought his eldest sister with him as she was very familiar with this whole affair with the twin.

I got on my evangelical soapbox and started spouting the message God had asked me to deliver, which in a nutshell was that this was the woman for him and he must stop his wild bachelor ways and settle down. In return, they explained that the twin had been a problem in the man's life for quite some time and there was nothing to discuss. Interestingly enough, even though he and his sister threw us out of his house and told us never to return, he gave me his phone number and promised to come to my house and hear the rest of what I had to say on another occasion. I was embarrassed and shamed, but I reinforced for myself the fact that I would always be a fool for God, no matter the cost to my life and ego.

The twin was distraught, to say the least, and was very reluctant to leave. I had to practically drag her out of the house to avoid further humiliation. I took her home and left her praying earnestly to God. Then I crashed out on the only piece of furniture, bar the empty fridge, I had. The bed.

The following Wednesday I called the aggresive twin's husband-to-be and invited him to the house. I told the twin not to be present but to wait in the bedroom so that he didn't think this was some kind of ploy to hook him but was a genuine request to be open to God's will. Reluctantly, she agreed.

Surprisingly, the man came. I prayed in tongues and, as was often the case, my prophesying abilities kicked in. I told him various things that shocked him, because I had no way of knowing them, and gave him God's instruction to basically be a real man and to stop playing at being a boy. To be honest, this man should have declared me insane and gotten the hell out of my sphere as fast as he could. Instead, he looked broken and thanked me humbly for my messages from God before he left.

The twin came out shaking, saying that she had felt the power of God as I had told the man God's will. Feeling empowered by having just delivered another accurate message from God, I told her that it was time for her to go. Again she lost it and insisted my task had not been completed. I told her that to the contrary, God had instructed me to deliver her to her husband after seven days and I had done just that. I told her that I had even gone beyond the call of duty by allowing her to stay longer and by making a further attempt to connect her with her husband-to-be. Time was now up. I told her to pack her bags so that I could take her back to her own house, where she lived with her brother. I told her that God had instructed me that she must find her own way and stop feeding off other people. Needless to say, she let me know that this was not what God was telling her. Still, there was nothing she could do.

That night, after dropping the aggresive twin off, I made a firm decision to have nothing to do with the Conniving Twins ever again. I didn't know how I was going to do it, but I knew my days of being a puppet and doing other people's "will" had to come to an end. Now it was just between God and me.

7

The call came and I found myself standing in court in front of a judge who finally pronounced me a divorced woman. The feeling is hard to describe, and I doubt I will ever experience such a sensation again. I think I have a real sense of how a wrongly convicted felon, having been imprisoned for life, feels when he is suddenly found innocent and released. I was free. This is what true freedom felt like. You have to know what being confined feels like to really appreciate the word *freedom*.

That wonderful high lasted for about half an hour. By the time I was back in my rented house in Johannesburg I was back to feeling lost and trapped. I couldn't see a way out. Although my share of the remaining money was to be released immediately, it was now only enough to pay the rent I owed my landlady.

There had been a time when I'd had a purpose and that sense of having a goal had made me work hard and reach a level of success I had never imagined possible. Somewhere along the line I had lost sight of that goal, and that had brought me to this place—a place of nothingness, a place where it was dark and every time I put out my hand to feel something solid I found myself groping thick, black air.

It was while I was sinking into this black, thick, endless abyss that I heard an insistent knock on my door. It was the landlady, dressed in her office suit, her tanned skin almost luminous as she waved her perfectly manicured nails at me and told me that I had a week to clear out. I couldn't think up any more ways to retaliate. I could give her what I had, then what? I was running on empty. I was a blank page, so much so that I couldn't even come up with a simple plan to get myself back on my feet. Calling my agent was beyond me. I couldn't contemplate auditions. Still I feared getting out there and being back in the limelight where "he", my now ex-husband, could find me. I didn't dare come out of the shadows. Not yet.

My self-esteem had sunk so low that I couldn't even conceive of finding other areas in my chosen profession to work in, like writing or producing or directing, all things I had done before, way back when I had courage and a vision. When the landlady left in her fancy Lamborghini, I dragged myself to my bed, threw myself upon it, spread my arms and legs wide in a star shape and began fervently to pray in tongues.

After some time I was convinced I heard other voices joining me in prayer. I was magically transported to this strange place that had a gigantic book on an altar, waiting for me. I opened it and was confronted with words. Only these were not words as I knew them. They were characters. I was looking at a language. God had decided to communicate with me again, but this time He was speaking to me through this language. I could only assume this was Aramaic, so beautiful were the characters on the pages of this gigantic book. As my invisible companions and I prayed, the words slid off the pages of the book and onto my body. I was lying in my star shape, back on the bed, as the words crawled across my body, covering me from head to toe. The only thought that came to mind was: *I am now the Word.*

It was the most incredible, delightful, insane vision I had ever had. I felt God had spoken. I leapt off the bed and ran into the empty living room and started screaming at the Almighty. I told Him that I would always be His servant. I told Him that He could go right ahead and continue to test me, but I would never walk away. I screamed at Him to come on and challenge me some more. "Come on!" I screamed. "Come on, Lord, is this all you've got? I can take it! My faith is unshakable, so bring it on!"

I prayed all day in this fashion and when the sun went down I scrambled for candles and continued in the dark and the cold. I even went out to the car to listen to some of the sermons I had on a CD. It was still cold and I still prayed. Even in the freezing shower the following morning, I no longer prayed as a victim. I challenged God to bring me fire and brimstone, to test my faith to the limit.

What was I doing? I think the words *tempting fate* come to mind here. I guess that's what I was doing.

For the next few days, I searched for somewhere to live. They all wanted a deposit and one month's rent. The best I could do was a month's rent. No one was interested. They all wanted their deposits. In the end, I decided the best thing to do was to spend a few nights in a cheap hotel, sell my car and find somewhere to live where I could then regroup and come up with a plan for my life. All this came to me through a haze of cheap wine and cigarette smoke. My only possessions—the bed and the fridge—would have to go to my friend, Joseph, at the petrol station.

The following day was spent looking for that cheap hotel room. I finally found one that I could afford to stay in for four, five days at the most. This meant that I had five days to sell my beloved green Mercedes. At least for the first time in a long time I had a plan. It was short term, but it was a start. I felt energised by it and that night I went to see Joseph to let him know that he could have my bed and fridge. It is always those who have so little who have the biggest hearts. Joseph's gratitude was humbling.

Unfortunately, Joseph's home was too small for the bed but he was thrilled with the fridge—apparently he and his wife had been longing for one for a very long time. Luckily he knew of a friend who would take my bed. He told me to come to the petrol station the following day so that I could meet his friend and he could arrange to come and collect the furniture from me.

My life in those two years after walking away from my poisonous marriage consisted of juggling, moving, owning, relinquishing . . . It was a great lesson in non-attachment. Nothing I owned I seemed to be able to keep, including a home.

The following day I met angel number two, Joseph's friend. He was a wonderful, middle-aged man with the kindest eyes. I guessed that Joseph had told him of my crazy situation because of the look he gave me. He thanked me profusely and told me that his daughter would now be able to sleep in her own bed. This in turn meant that he and his wife would have their bedroom to themselves because his daughter could share a room with her brother. As I listened to Joseph's friend I felt deep rage well up in the pit of my stomach. In such a vast land with such great riches families should not have to live like sardines packed in a tin can. It infuriated me that the leaders of the country had forgotten why they had fought for so long for equal rights. It seemed to me that they had lost sight of who they were fighting for while they enjoyed dinner with Queen Elizabeth in Buckingham Palace. In Joseph and the angel I saw no bitterness, just a quiet need to live as best they could and to provide for their families. Beautiful spirits, beautiful.

Joseph's friend had come in a small van that would just about take the double bed. After we had all helped load the bed he told us that he would come back for the fridge and take it to Joseph's house. Then he suddenly turned to me and asked if, since he had to come back for the fridge, I would please accompany him to his home because he knew his wife would love to meet me and thank me for the bed. How could I refuse? With a full heart I got into the angel's van.

The neighbours, who were always peeping from behind their net curtains, must have breathed a huge sigh of relief when they saw the van leaving with my furniture. The crazy woman who talked to herself and regularly screamed passionately at God was finally leaving.

The angel lived in a new government-built house. On entering this maze of low-cost housing, again I was overwhelmed by a feeling of rage. I couldn't believe how little regard the government had for the ordinary people of South Africa. These houses were minute and built closely together, almost on top of one another. There were no parks or greenery, just concrete cells. That is the only way I can find to describe them.

When we walked into the angel's house I thought I was going to faint. The living room, kitchen and dining room were basically one room. His wife and daughter greeted me warmly and his wife thanked me profusely for the bed. Smiling, the angel led me to their bedroom and showed me where the bed would go, which was basically the whole room. The thrill and excitement on their faces made me want to laugh and cry at the same time. It was only a bed; I wish it could have been a house.

The angel called a neighbour over and they offloaded the bed. The neighbour was most impressed and expressed his envy at his friend's good fortune. It was like I had given them gold.

Finally, the angel motioned for me to get back into the van because it was time to go. As I hugged and kissed his wife, she pressed a R100 note into my hand. I tried to protest—I knew that this was food for their family—but she shook her head and said that the angel had told her I was struggling and that they wanted to give me something in return for all the years of joy I had brought them while I was on television.

My legs could barely carry me. What can I say? This is the character of the ordinary South African.

8

I sat in the hotel room and stared out of the window at my car. It was parked in the hotel car park, bedding piled high on the back seat. The award from the Fespaco film festival was on the table next to me. My suitcase was at my feet. These were all the possessions I had in the whole world. Strange, I didn't feel I needed anything else, and even some of what I did have I felt could go. The award only stayed with me because Quezi had told me to keep it forever. Farai had cleared off with all my other awards—goodness knows why, unless he intended to sell them to feed his drug habit. Sometimes I wish I had them, just so I could see where I have been and who I have become as a result of all my successes and failures.

Funnily enough, Farai had left the photograph of us with Tata Mandela behind. I had given it to the church charity after I had taken what remained of my belongings from the house because Farai was in the photograph. All I could think of when I looked at it was how irritated I had been that day when he had insisted on taking a photograph with the great man. I just felt he could have handled it better.

All I had to show for the world I had left behind and was now hiding from was a Mercedes, a duvet, two small bags, a suitcase, an award, my cellphone and a handbag.

I went to bed with the thought that I would go to Joseph's petrol station the following day, park and see if I could get any buyers for the car.

I was up extremely early as if I had a job to go to. Little did I know that trying to sell old Gertie would become my full-time job. Yes, that was the name of my beloved green Mercedes. My eldest sister had baptised her long before we learned from my mother that this was

140

what they used to call my grandmother: Gertie, which was short for Gertrude.

My mother was in Cape Town. She had no idea what a loser her daughter had become and I had no intention of burdening her with this knowledge. I was kind of angry with my family. I felt let down by them. I was bitter that they had all disliked Farai but had stayed away from me instead of talking to me and trying to help me through a situation that had left me feeling powerless.

You see that? You see how disappointment in ourselves can sometimes be so hard to swallow that we pile all our toxicity onto others, especially our loved ones? I chose my circumstances, but in part I blamed my family. Not my mother. She had done her part by creating a path that had given me every opportunity to live a successful, happy life. With my mother, I just felt guilt, guilt that expressed itself in my inability to communicate with her. She used to try and call me, but I could rarely bring myself to speak to her. When we did speak, I was distant. I had nothing to tell her.

What I didn't know was that my mother's days were numbered—in a year she would no longer be in this world. If I'd known that, would I have done things differently? "I don't know," is the true answer to that question. "I don't know."

Still, I am eternally grateful to Quezi for sticking with me till I woke up and broke out of my toxic marriage, for putting herself in the line of fire in order for me to see what was really going on in my space. That is what family members should do for one another, right? At the time she was going through her own hell, and as far as I could, with the limited resources I had at my disposal, I helped her to keep afloat. Even if it was barely afloat.

Joseph was at the petrol station early too.

I told him my plan and he said that he would send people over to take a look at the car as they came in to fill up. I sat in Gertie all day. From time to time, I surfaced for a smoke, letting people see me in the hope that they would want to talk, then I would throw them my sales pitch.

I kept forgetting that my face was known to so many. Most of the time, all people wanted to talk about was why I had left *Generations* and when was I intending to come back onto their screens.

I had to hold back the desire to beg them to forget my celebrity status for one second and buy my car so that I would not end up on the street. They, of course, were oblivious. Sure, it was strange that I had bedding piled up in the back of my car, but as far as they were concerned I was a successful actress. Little did they know that I would have sold them the duvet if one of them had asked. I needed cash; I was running out of it fast.

It was surreal watching people getting on with their lives while mine felt like it had halted. Stopped. It was strange looking at the world that I had once been a part of, going about my business, and realising that it was now completely alien to me. There had been a time when it was "normal" and I didn't imagine there was any other way to be. I didn't really think about people like Joseph, people who filled my car with petrol. I never wondered about their lives and the challenges they and their families might be facing. Never wondered how they got around, where they lived, what their philosophies of life might be. Now Joseph was the only thing that made sense in my world.

Five days came to a close very, very fast. In no time it was time for me to leave the hotel. I stared at a small picture of Jesus I had acquired. In it He was wearing the crown of thorns.

I felt very close to Him at that moment because I felt that I was definitely donning my own crown of thorns. I was facing the unthinkable: homelessness. That happened to other people, not to me, Pamela, daughter of Bax and Corah Nomvete. The time had come to face the fact that I had completely run out of money and would have to sleep in my car, the one I was trying to sell in order to rent a house or flat. For now, my beautiful, old, faithful, green Mercedes was going to shelter me before she sacrificed herself in order for me to get back on my feet.

I checked out of the hotel and sat in the car, frozen for a few minutes. Where was I going to park the car and sleep that night? I knew I couldn't stay in the hotel car park. There would be too many questions. Suddenly it was as if someone—God as far as I was concerned at this point in my life—had tapped me on the shoulder. I looked up and noticed a petrol station across the road. It had a small parking area that was somewhat sheltered. I was looking at my new home.

I found a spot at the edge of the parking area, so I could have some privacy. I sat there and searched for small change so that I could get a cup of coffee before I drove to the other petrol station to resume trying to sell Gertie. I was worried because the petrol was getting really low and I reckoned that although I could get there and back that day, the following day would be a problem. I began to sift through my phone, looking for people I could borrow money from. It was so hard. I couldn't ask for any more money from my family—I had used up all those favours. There were times when I had borrowed from my mother and my brother, and I still owed them. Now I was turning to the kindness of strangers.

Unfortunately, the people who would have had absolutely no problem with lending me money—in fact, would have insisted that I take a loan from them—were going through tough times themselves. I realise now that almost everyone had been living beyond his or her means, trying to keep up with life in the fast lane in the new South Africa. We all couldn't get enough. We wanted more and more and more!

I was out of the rat race—gone were the Champagne lunches, the designer clothes and the visits to the top hairdressers—but I had almost nothing to show for having been in it. I had no money and no home. The funny thing was I hadn't been brought up to covet expensive things. My parents were excellent money managers. I guess hard times taught them to be that way. At that moment I needed my father's wisdom (even though I knew deep down that had he been alive I would never have let him know I had reached such an all-time low). I mean, I couldn't even tell my mother what was going on. I was hiding from everybody and yet here I was, centre stage and destitute.

There was also a part of me, however, that was enjoying living simply, enjoying not having to participate in pointless conversations about success, money and the next project. In a strange way, even though I was under tremendous pressure and in pain, lost and horribly depressed, there was this tiny glimmer of happiness. Somehow, with no material goods to speak of and a diminishing reputation, I felt liberated. Yes, liberated. No ties; nothing to protect or preserve; just surviving hour to hour, day to day.

I realised that in my life, possessions had tended to imprison me, and when I walked out of my marriage, away from the house, my job and the limelight, I was desperately trying to shake myself free.

I wanted and find true happiness. How curious that it might just be found in this world of non-attachment to anything: people, status, reputation. This thought was exhilarating, almost holy.

There was something missing, though—a sense of responsibility.

Being responsible for nothing felt fantastic! This was how anarchists must feel, I told myself. This was what having nothing to lose felt like. This was what feeling valueless could do to one.

What I didn't realise is that I was also killing my desire to live, because by completely disengaging I had lost my sense of purpose. My world was shrinking daily. They were the most confusing emotions I have ever experienced. It was as if I was pulling myself apart bit by bit in order to figure something out, only I had no idea what.

9

After much deliberation, I decided not to drive to Joseph's petrol station that day but to rather take a drive to a car dealer I had spotted just around the corner from where I was. This journey would mean I would use up less petrol and my spirits were somewhat lifted by the idea that they might just buy the car then and there. Filled with this glimmer of hope, I noticed that the area where I had parked the car was quite beautiful. There was a big tree sheltering Gertie and the sun shining in the deep, blue, African sky was strong and bright.

For a second a positive thought flashed across my mind: *That's my future. Strong and bright like the African sun.*

It was only a moment, a flicker, and then the thought vanished.

At the car dealership I sat patiently as an employee looked over the car. As luck would have it, while I waited I received a call from one of the good Samaritans I had asked for money. He said that he could help me out and we arranged to meet later that day. Maybe my luck was beginning to change. Maybe this was God's sign that my trials were over.

The dealer returned and offered me a ridiculous price for the car.

He saw my deep disappointment. Perhaps it moved him because he went on to advise me not to go to a dealer if I wanted to get a good price for the car. He said I should rather try to sell it privately because a dealer will always calculate his commission and take off money for any work he may have to do on the car.

Disheartened, I made my way back to the petrol station. To cheer myself up, I tried to focus on the fact that I was going to pick up some money later in the day, that I could then use to fill the car with petrol and get some food. But then what? Broke again, unless I could make a sale.

My phone rang again. It was a woman who was a good friend of a friend of mine. She had heard that I was trying to sell my car and she had a brother who was a mechanic. She felt he might be interested in buying the car. The great thing about good friends is that, even if they can't help you out, they will try to find other solutions to your problems. I told her to please pass on my details to her brother.

Again the phone rang and it was the mechanic. He asked me a couple of questions about the car and at the end he gave me an amount I could work with. Perfect. I had done it! I had sold my car. Then came the hitch. He was an hour out of Johannesburg. Even if I made it to his place, how would I make it back with all my belongings? He was unable to get me back into town, so I was on my own. After a lot of pointless negotiation, he told me that he would come up with a plan and call me that night. Brilliant! I was still hopeful. How complicated could it be to get me transport back to Johannesburg? The money I was due to get that night would see me through until I was paid for Gertie.

I waited for the mechanic to call all day while I walked aimlessly in and around the petrol station. I noticed the attendants giving me curious stares, but they left me alone.

Unable to stand the wait, I drove to Joseph's petrol station to pick up a couple of cigarettes. When I got there, I noticed several minibustaxis parked in a back area. Out of the blue I decided to approach oneof the drivers. They were scary individuals, bereft of any charm, but when you have nothing to lose you become fearless. That survival instinct, the one that guides you on where to go or not go, is switched off. Again, my well-known face meant that people were more open to communicating with me, even if it was only out of curiosity. The driver broke out into a smile when I approached him and listened as I pointed to the car, asking if he was interested in buying it. He said that he might be but that he didn't have money. I was stunned. These guys collected wads of cash daily. It never occurred to me that they were collecting it for someone else and what they were left with at the end of the day wasn't much. Life on the street was a huge education for me.

The driver came and looked the car over, then told me he would be back later with his wife. She had a business and would have the cash for me if she agreed to buy the car. I arranged to see him later that night after I had collected my own money.

I got my daily supply of cigarettes from Joseph with the promise that I would pay for them the following day. Joseph refused. He said he would not take any money from me. He said that the only thing he wanted from me was to get back on my feet and start living again. Who made the mistake of thinking angels were unearthly beings with wings? For me, they are very much of this world.

Before I knew it, it was dark and Joseph's shift was over, which meant that it was time for me to meet my friend.

I climbed into my car and set off.

When I reached the place we had agreed to meet, Themba Ndaba was waiting for me. This was my old friend, the young man who had saved me from Hillbrow in my early days in South Africa. Now here he was, helping me out again. My life seemed to have come full circle. Themba told me that he was living in a cottage about forty-five minutes out of Johannesburg. He had been one of the people God had directed me to pray for and, sweetly, he thanked me for my prayers, adding that as a result of our session he and his estranged wife were making amends. He told me that he felt what I was doing was a good thing and it worked. I was grateful for his encouragement and mentioned that I was looking for somewhere to live and would be interested in taking over his cottage once he vacated it, having returned to his wife. He promised he would be in touch.

That night, with a full tank of petrol and having eaten a pie with a hot coffee, I did something I hadn't done for quite some time since I had begun my life on the streets. I prayed.

Soon after that, I got a phone call from the taxi driver, asking me to meet with him and his wife the following day at five pm. Even though my pockets were empty, life felt promising. It was all opening up again.

At five pm I was at Joseph's, ready to meet with my prospective buyers. After about a fifteen-minute wait, I saw the taxi driver making his way over to me with a large, well-dressed woman. He introduced her as his wife. As she greeted me, she had a faint smile on her lips. She told me that she couldn't believe she was meeting "Ntsiki" from television. I tried to take her comment in my stride but couldn't help feeling somewhat despondent. What if that was the real reason for this meeting? His wife wanted to meet a television star. At that moment I wasn't interested in praise; it was her money I needed. I tried to brush over the excited fan moment and lead them to the car, but she wouldn't stop staring at me—literally inspecting me from head to toe—as her husband looked over the car. She asked me suspiciously why I was selling Gertie. I lied and told her I was buying a new one. She asked why I didn't just trade it in with a dealer. I told her that I had a great fondness for the car and that I wanted to make sure it went to a good owner. She seemed fairly satisfied with this answer but continued to inspect me closely. There was absolutely no subtlety in her action.

Finally, her husband came over and they spoke rapidly to each other in Zulu. As always, I regretted deeply that I had never learned the language. At the end of their deliberations, she barked a price at me that was totally unsatisfactory. I tried to negotiate with her, but she absolutely refused to budge. Even her husband tried to get her to compromise on the price, but she barked at him too and basically told me to take the offer or leave it. Then she walked away, leaving me high, dry and desperate. The adoring fan moment, if that's what you could call it, was over. This was business, Ntsiki or no Ntsiki.

Her husband followed her and they had another conversation. He came back looking very sheepish and asked for my phone number. He told me that he really wanted the car and would get back to me the following day. I had no choice but to agree. I felt sick; my stomach began to knot and I felt like I was about to bring up the pie that I had eaten earlier. In desperation I asked the taxi driver for his number, thinking I could force his hand by pushing for an answer if he didn't get back to me.

We exchanged numbers and I drove back to my temporary home base in order to regroup and figure out what I was going to do.

10

I woke up feeling weak, depressed and cold. What a long winter this had turned out to be. *Why was nothing moving in my life?* I kept praying to God, but nothing moved. I was still stuck in no-man's-land.

I had the last remnants of the money I had been given the night before, enough for a cup of coffee. When I walked into the petrol station shop after my daily birdbath in its modest washrooms, the attendants and cashier fell silent. I ordered my coffee, but when I went to pay for it, the cashier told me that one of the petrol attendants had said that he would pay for it. I was stunned. Speechless. Moved. I stupidly asked her which of the attendants it was that had performed such an overwhelmingly kind act. The cashier pointed him out to me. I went over and thanked him as I sipped the pipinghot coffee. He graciously accepted my thanks, then got on with his work.

It is so amazing when people do things purely from the heart. This man had absolutely no agenda—he just wanted to help me out with a cup of early morning coffee. I could not remember the last time that this had happened to me. I was so used to being suspicious of people's motives. Inevitably, if they wanted to hang around me they wanted something from me. It was as if somehow they thought that my fame meant that I could wave a magic wand and make their dreams come true. In contrast, this was an unconditional act of kindness.

Feeling like the world was not such a hostile place after all, I placed a call to the mechanic. I still hadn't heard from him. His phone rang and rang and rang. I left a message, knowing full well that I would probably never hear from him again.

Next, I called the taxi driver, who answered his phone and confirmed that he was still interested in the car and promised to call me that evening. My confidence had returned somewhat, so I decided to visit one of the largest taxi ranks in Johannesburg. It was in Randburg, which was a five-minute drive from where I was.

Arriving at the taxi rank, I parked the car and stepped out. The place was a hive of activity: Kombis everywhere, long lines of people waiting to get to various destinations.

I walked towards an area that looked like a resting place for drivers. At first I stood nervously at the door, working up the courage to approach one of the men inside. However, it wasn't long before my well-known face got their attention. I mentioned that I had a car to sell and asked if any of them was interested. They stared at me blankly and then kind of got on with their conversations. One or two said that they would ask around and I should come back the following day.

Feeling rather despondent and embarrassed, I left them and returned to my car, trying to figure out what my next move should be. As I sat there and begged God to please give me some guidance, to open a way for me, two gentlemen came and knocked on my window. They looked terribly serious till I stepped out.

They said that they had heard that I was trying to sell my car and they had come to look it over. My immediate reaction was that they looked like two mafia henchmen—probably not far from the truth— but at least they seemed quite serious about the car. They asked me to open the bonnet and then proceeded to check the engine over again and again, consulting each other every step of the way. Finally, they asked me for my cell number and said that they would be in touch. Then they were gone.

I decided to get out of the area because I was attracting a lot of attention and returned to base. The only option left was to wait for someone to come through for me. I had done all I could.

I sat staring out of the window, my mind unable to focus on anything. I couldn't see a way ahead. I knew it was temporary, but I had no idea how I would get out of the situation in which I found myself. Suddenly, a man standing at my window blocked the sun from my view. He called me by my television character name, Ntsiki, very politely, so I responded. He said that he was the manager of the petrol station and that he wanted to talk to me. My heart sank. *This is it*, I thought. *I am going to be thrown off the property. Understandably. I am sure they must have rules about cars being parked at the station for only a certain length of time.*

I sheepishly got out of the car, ready to sink to my knees and beg for mercy.

He asked me directly what was going on. He said that he and his colleagues had observed me over the time I had been there and wanted to know if they could help. I almost wept at his concern for my welfare. I couldn't believe the size of some people's hearts.

It was overwhelming.

I wasn't going to insult his kind intelligence by making up some story that would help me save face. Instead I told him my circumstances had taken a turn for the worse. I told him that I was not going to go into how I found myself in the situation he was witnessing, but yes, I was homeless and living in my car that I was trying to sell in order to start a new life.

He couldn't believe what he was hearing. He asked me the same question Joseph had asked me—why I didn't go and ask my "friends" from the soap opera to help me out. I told him, just as I had told Joseph, that what he was suggesting was so much easier said than done, that when you are part of the club people are there for you, but when you are outside that circle and have nothing to offer, no one is interested. When you are down, people who are riding the wave take every opportunity to kick you to the curb.

As an example of just how prevalent this is in human nature, let me share something that happened many years after this period in South Africa, when I was back in England. There was a woman in England, an old acquaintance, who was a director. At some point she started to talk to me about a project she was working on with John Kani, then she suddenly went quiet. I didn't hear from her for quite some time and when I tried to make contact with her, she was very cool. Eventually, she intimated to me that John Kani was telling people that I'd had some kind of nervous breakdown. I was shocked and profoundly disappointed in this icon for trying to discredit me, even when I was out of the country. Unfortunately, this is human nature. He had no idea what had happened to me, but because I had not been willing to meet his demands he chose to try to halt my progress. At the time I wondered how many more people were jumping on that bandwagon.

It was this kind of reaction that prevented me from asking for help, I told my concerned enquirer. I told him, hard as it was, that the one person I could trust was myself, and I was kind of hoping God was on my side, even though there were times when I wasn't sure of that either.

He bent his head and shook it in deep sympathy. I thanked him for his kindness and for restoring my faith in the human spirit. In response he said that if there was anything they could do for me, I should just ask. He asked me how much I was selling the car for and said he would let the customers know that it was for sale..

I did not know what to say to this man.

I collapsed back in the car and thanked God for the incredible experience I was having. When I'd had everything, I was never in a position to have this kind of interaction with people. This is where my real loyalty should have always lain. Those who were constantly demanding my loyalty because they paid me or because they were from the "right" social structures did not, as far as I was concerned at that moment, deserve my loyalty.

The people I was meeting now were beautiful, they made me feel that life was worth living. I wanted to work for them. These people were keeping me alive.

A few minutes later, the manager returned. Under his arm he was carrying a few pieces of A4 paper and in his hand he had a coffee. I opened the door and he handed me the coffee, saying that he had bought it for me, to keep me warm. He then proceeded to show me that the paper was makeshift *For Sale* signs he had created on his computer, describing the car and the price I was asking. He pasted them on my windows in the back of the car and on the windscreen. Satisfied, he said he would send people over. Again, he had left me speechless and full. That cup of coffee I know came out of his meagre wage.

In that moment, I was overwhelmed by the feeling that I absolutely loved the people of South Africa.

11

Filled with a deep sense of gratitude, I was consumed with a desire to go and worship. There was a very big and very popular church just around the corner and so I made my way there.

When I entered the huge edifice and saw people deep in prayer that evening, I was moved to that place once again, sure that God's voice was one I could hear. As the pastor bent his head in prayer and invited us all to do the same, the thought that this was a church hit me: this was God's house. Here they would house me and feed me while I got back on my feet.

After the service, I went to one of the ushers and explained my situation. He pointed out one of the younger pastors and told me to talk to him. As I made my way through the crowd to the pastor, a large man in what looked like a security guard's uniform came up to me and asked me where I was going. I explained that I wanted to have a word with one of the pastors. He asked me if I was a member of the church. I told him that I was not but I thought God's house was open to all people. He confirmed that it was but asked me to become a member as then I would be permitted to talk to any of the pastors at any time. All I remember saying is: "Brother, I am desperate." The look in my eyes must have reflected that desperation, because he let me go in a manner that indicated that next time, if I came back as a non-member, he would not let me in.

Slightly unsettled by this member business, I carried on with my mission to speak to the priest. When I reached him, I got straight to the point. I asked him if the church would help me either by lending me some money or providing me with temporary accommodation. He turned me down flat on both counts, telling me that what I was asking for was not part of the work of the church. First I would have to become a member of the church, and only then would they see if there was any accommodation available. And even if there was, he added, it would be some distance out of town.

There it was again, *if* I was a member I would, maybe, have access to all the treasures of heaven. And there I was, thinking that we were all God's children.

I was reminded instantly of what had happened to my father's family when my grandfather died. You know, when they threw my grandmother and her five children out onto the streets. I looked at the church very differently from that day on and wondered about its ethics.

I left that building certain that I would never find the heart of God in a church; I was experiencing the true nature of the human spirit on the streets among people who could barely rub two cents together.

In my frustration, I decided to give the church one more chance by returning to the warehouse church. The warehouse was still there, but the building was deserted. You couldn't tell that it had ever been a church.

I decided to drive around the suburbs and look for prospective buyers for Gertie. I drove past one of the huge complexes that housed terrified middle-class businesspeople behind its high walls. I decided to approach the security guard who was manning the gates of the fortress and see if he was interested in buying a car. He said that he was, but the only way he would be able to afford it was if he asked his uncle, who had some money, to help him. There was something about this man that was so hopeful.

I agreed to meet up with Peter after work the next day and take him to his house where I would talk to his uncle.

The following evening, having collected Peter, we made our way into the dark, slushy undergrowth that is Diepsloot. There are many stories of how people have been robbed and killed just driving past this place. Now I was going into the heart of it in my green Mercedes Benz.

When we reached Peter's home, it was pitch black. Before we entered, he stopped for a few minutes to speak with another young man. As we entered, I noticed his friend had remained by the car. Peter explained that he had told him to watch over it as people had been known to lose parts of their vehicles when they left them standing in the compounds of Diepsloot.

Peter's house was pitch black, bar the faint light from a flickering candle. I could just about make out a woman sitting on the floor and a middle-aged man in an armchair. The woman, who Peter introduced as his mother, pulled out a small stool for me to sit on. As I took a seat I noticed a small coffee table, a paraffin stove and a curtain that acted as a door to what I could only imagine was a bedroom. My hunch was confirmed when Peter pulled the curtain back to go into the room and put away his stuff, revealing a huge double bed. I could not help myself. I asked him where he and his mother slept and he told me that they all slept in the one room. I suddenly felt very hot. Once again, I was angry with the leaders of our country. The newspapers every day were full of horror stories about young children, some actual infants, being molested and raped. If you left people to live as if they didn't matter, without dignity, then you had to accept the consequences. It began to feel to me as if the people of Diepsloot had been forgotten.

The man in the armchair—Peter's uncle—asked about the car. I told him as much as I could. Peter added that it was in good condition— he said that he could tell when I was bringing him to the house. The uncle asked my price and when I told him, he said he would bring the money the following morning at ten am. Peter's mother, who was a domestic worker, said that she had the day off, so she would also be at the house to receive both of us.

I left Peter's home, grateful for the fact that at last I had found a buyer and furious that there was a whole side of South Africa that was unknown by many of the people I had once rubbed shoulders with on a daily basis. They employed domestic workers but had no idea where they were coming from every morning and going home to every night: the armpit of the world. These women were heroes in the true sense of the word. Warriors.

I returned the next day to find a pot of tea and an egg sandwich waiting for me. Peter's mother said that he had told her what had happened to me and that she wanted me to have at least one good meal that day. I knew that she was taking food out of her own mouth to feed me. This was church to me. Here I could worship and give praise to true holiness, here in the heart of the human being.

It was dawning on me that when you encounter a real human being, that is when you encounter divinity.

Peter's uncle never turned up, but it didn't matter.

12

I woke up to two men peering in through my window. I was feeling tired and cramped, the norm for me during those days. These were the two mafia types who had looked the car over before. *How did they know I was here?*

I disentangled myself and slowly got out of the car, feeling rather crusty and unkempt because I hadn't yet had a chance to go to the washroom. My visitors said that they wanted to test drive the car. I wasn't about to argue, so I reached in for a small bag that had my toiletries and a change of underwear in it and handed them the keys. Mad, I know, but I had grown careless, tired from living on the street. Imagine how people feel who are condemned to that life forever.

Half an hour later they were back and—after explaining all the work that they would have to do on the car to fix it up—offered me a sum that was way below my asking price. However, they were offering cash, which meant I could go immediately to the Magaliesberg and pay a deposit and rent for two months. I agreed to the sale.

The next thing was to get the police to witness the signing over of the car with its correct documentation. There was only one person I could call on at this point to help me get from the police station to the Magaliesberg and that person was Chichi Letswalo. I agreed to meet the gentlemen at the police station in Sandton, which was the nearest cop shop to Chichi's house.

When they drove off I felt that this was the turning point in my life. I still had no idea how to proceed, but at least I would have the space and time to think and pray and come up with some answers. One thing that was clear was that I had to get out of South Africa for a while so I could look at her with fresh eyes.

On my way to Sandton I stopped off at the petrol station and told my friends that I was leaving. We thanked one another profusely for our friendship and I knew in that moment that even if we were not fortunate enough to meet again, we would treasure our time together for as long as there was breath in our bodies.

Sitting in the Sandton police station hours later, waiting for the buyers and Chichi, I thought back over the two bizarre weeks I had just lived through. Whichever way I looked at it, my life had expanded tenfold as a result of this surreal period. But how had I ended up in the predicament in which I had found myself? This is a question I continue to ask myself, only now it doesn't seem that important because of the ordinary people with whom I made a real connection. I recall that the manager of the petrol station, when I told him about my situation, said he was sorry for my troubles but he was so happy that they had brought me to him because now he got to see Ntsiki every day in the flesh. My dad always used to say, "Isn't life grand?" Now I think I know what he meant.

I chuckled to myself while remembering another strange incident at the petrol station. I was standing with one of the attendants one afternoon when this huge monstrosity of a car pulled in. He was busy telling me that these particular vehicles consumed ridiculous amounts of fuel when a woman climbed out of the car. Recognising her, the attendant exclaimed that here was one of my friends from television. Sure enough she was one of the actresses from *Muvhango*, the television series I had been in after *Generations*.

Spotting me, the actress came sauntering over and greeted me warmly. She briefly took in my dishevelled appearance before launching into a diatribe about the series and all the politics surrounding it. In the middle of her tirade a young Asian gentleman, totally distraught, rushed over to us and asked if we could give him R10 so that he could put petrol in his car. He told us that he had been busy filling it up when he had noticed that the tank was leaking. With no other choice, he had to fix the leak there and then, and he had used up all his cash doing just this. He said that he needed to buy fuel to get home and that R10 would be enough.

I immediately responded by telling him that if I had it, it would be his. The actress, meanwhile, shook her head. The young man left distressed. The actress then began to talk angrily about how the Asian man's request for R10 was most probably a scam and how she was not about to be taken for a fool.

Sitting in the police station, having lived for two weeks on the streets in my car, I thought that once upon a time I probably would have felt just like her. But on that day I knew exactly what that young man was going through, if he was genuine. My attitude had changed. Even if I had felt that there was only a fifty per cent chance that he was genuine, that would have made me hand over R10. If it was a scam, well, he would have to live with his conscience.

As soon as Chichi and the gentlemen arrived we went through the whole process, which went smoothly. With all the paperwork completed, I emptied Gertie's contents into Chichi's car and reluctantly handed over the keys to her new owners. I loved that car; it had saved my life. The men thanked me and drove off, looking very pleased with their new purchase.

Chichi explained to me that while I had been signing the papers, the main man had told her—in Zulu—that he had decided to buy the car because he could see that things had gone wrong in Ntsiki's life and he wanted to help. That is why these men had returned to buy the car. Even mafia types have hearts.

Four years later I went on holiday to Johannesburg, and on the day before I left I went to Sandton to have lunch with my sister-in-law. When we separated, I was strolling along, looking at the taxis parked on the side of the road and thinking I should book one of them to take me to the airport the following day. From the corner of my eye I saw a green Mercedes and my first thought was: *That looks just like Gertie!*

At that moment, I saw the number plate, and it was Gertie! I ran to the cab and banged on his window. The driver rolled it down and I asked him if he made trips to the airport. He said he did, so we exchanged numbers and he agreed to pick me up the following day. Just before we parted, he asked me if I recognised my car. Surprised he knew it was mine, I affirmed that I did and then asked him how he knew. He said that I had sold it to him and his friend and they were in the taxi business, as I could see. I told him I was so grateful to have had the opportunity to meet him again and thanked him for saving my life. We were both moved and the next day I was taken to the airport in my beautiful green Mercedes that had been my home for two weeks. She had served me so well and with such loyalty. What a special car. I don't think any more can be said on the subject, do you?

13

The cottage Themba had vacated and I now occupied was situated in the middle of nowhere. I had a few clothes, my award and a couple of books to my name, but I was now living in a fully furnished one-bedroom cottage with a washing machine, television and DVD player. There was furniture! It was as if everything I had lost had somehow come back to me.

The cottage was in a valley surrounded by the harsh, almost angry landscape of the Magaliesberg mountains—truly one of the most powerful places I have ever seen. This is where I was to reflect on what my next move would be. The money was going to run out—and soon—so I had to come up with a plan.

The owners of the cottage were English, funnily enough, and were very pleasant. The two other cottages were owned by an Afrikaans family comprised of extremely warm and wonderful people.

It was interesting that there was a DVD player because I found myself watching *Sometimes in April* over and over again with a feeling of nostalgia. I kept replaying a conversation I'd had with Idris Elba in my mind. He'd told me that I should think about LA. He'd said that he reckoned that I could penetrate the industry in the States. At the time he'd said this I was knee deep in my horrendous life as Mrs Sapiens and couldn't see my way ahead, but I remember feeling grateful that he'd taken the time to open me up to that possibility. I even hired *The Wire*, for which he was known in those days.

Somehow, this period saw me awakening to the idea that I had a skill, and that skill was as an actress, and this is where I needed to start with rebuilding my life.

Chichi would visit often and we would cook for each other and encourage each other in pursuing our dreams, rather like I had done with my friends at the petrol station. We prayed a lot and, as she was also going through a transition in her life, we worked on finding a way to stay alive and find our purpose.

Chichi finally decided that she was going to go to the US and I decided that the best course of action for me would be to return to England and find my footing there. I'd had a career there once, so maybe I could build one again, even though I was forty-five years old. It was a challenge, but I was ready for it! I had come to South Africa empty-handed, become famous, been married, divorced and lost everything, but I was still alive. I had gone full circle.

Chichi sold her car and most of her belongings in no time and not long after that we were embracing and saying goodbye—her friend, who was driving her to the airport, made a pit stop at my cottage at her request. That night when I prayed, I was convinced I heard God give me an instruction. He said that I was to expect a call and my response to that call was to just say "Yes." This is no word of a lie: two days later I got a call from Quezi, telling me that she had received an email from a director. He had been looking for me because he had written a part for me in a television series that he was shooting in the next week or so. He wanted to know if I would do the job. I remembered the instruction from God, so I just said "Yes."

That is the job that bought my ticket to London in December 2007.

I contacted a couple of friends to help me find somewhere temporary and cheap to stay. I had my last phone call with my mother, who was now very ill, and who I was not able to afford to go and see. I told her I was going to England and she seemed to give me her blessing.

I arrived in London on 23 December.

My friend had found me a room at the top of a dingy house in South London. On 24 December I attended midnight mass with my friend and was filled with my mother's spirit. I spoke to her and told her to let go and be with Dad, her soul mate, so she could be happy. On the morning of 25 December, Christmas Day, my friend came to tell me that my mother had passed in the early hours of the morning. I was grateful.

My friend's family very kindly invited me to spend Christmas with them, which was quite wonderful because I could tell that they really didn't understand what was going on with me and were trying as hard as they could not to judge.

I was unable to speak to my sister, Sheila, who lived in London because I was still so angry with my family. And so with very little money, I paid a ridiculous amount to stay in the hole of a room that my friend had found me while I looked for work.

One day, I sat smoking outside the grey, filthy window that was mine and asked Jesus to come and see me. When I was sure I could feel His presence, I asked Him to show me this law He spoke of, the one He called God's law. I told Him that once I found out what that law was I would finally be able to live a fulfilling and meaningful life and maybe discover true happiness.

Not long after, when my money was running out and my landlady was becoming increasingly abusive, an old friend of mine invited me to stay with her and her husband. It was because of them that I was able to make contact with an agent, one of the best in London.

It was a strange time because I realised that my friend had a different life and there was no way I could fit into it, so we parted on bad terms. I had to accept my life was shifting into a completely different dimension. I finally made contact with my sister and we ended up getting a bond together on a beautiful two-bedroom flat that I now live in.

In 2009, four years after I had walked away from Farai and my life with him, seeing him only once after that—on that horrible day in the lawyer's office—I received a phone call about him. One morning, while having coffee in South London, a friend called and informed me Farai had been very ill with lymphatic cancer for some time and that it had finally claimed his life.

My friend's message was as follows: "The only reason I am telling you this is that I wanted you to know you are now truly free."

I thought of Hilda. I guess Farai's death wish had finally been granted. I can only hope he finds happiness wherever he is in our fine universe.

Epilogue

When I take a step back and examine all the ingredients in the crazy conundrum that my life in South Africa became, I realise that all the challenges that greet me are an opportunity for me to keep asking "What am I here to do? What is my purpose?"

I have come to understand that purpose and the desire to empower others often arise in the face of what may seem to be insurmountable obstacles. The Sapienses and the baptism by fire they took me through is the very thing that gave me the impetus to identify what my purpose might be.

I went back to the UK to heal, I wanted to look at South Africa, my "homeland", from a safe distance. I needed the anonymity that Queen Elizabeth II's terrain had always afforded me.

And that's just what I got: anonymity.

In the UK I returned to just being an actress, without the celebrity label attached.

It was like being born again. All of my old persona—what I had thought of as me for the last thirteen years—was washed away. I didn't care if I remained invisible to the populace; I just needed to get to know ME.

Who was I? Why was I here? I mean *here*, in the world. What was my purpose?

It was strange returning to the career path I thought I had left behind forever, but, a year after returning to the UK, I was performing on the stages of the Royal Court, the Royal Shakespeare Company, the Royal National Theatre. It was crazy. I worked nonstop but things were different, my perspective had changed.

Interacting with my fellow thespians, I no longer hungered for the acknowledgement that success offered us.

I wanted so much more.

I had seen where this could lead.

As I painstakingly put my life back together, piece by piece, brick by brick, the core energy that consumed me resembled that of those beautiful souls that had saved my life in Johannesburg.

It began to dawn on me that if it hadn't been for my journey through "tinsel town" South Africa, if it hadn't been for the vicious desperation displayed by the Sapienses and many others who believed that money and reputation were their salvation, I may never have come to this point. The point of knowing there was so much more to life than the adulation and accolades that a career like mine might bring.

The Sapienses greed had driven me to material and emotional destitution. Not only had I lost everything financially, I had lost my pride. I had felt consumed by a sense of shame and failure.

What brought me back?

Faith in the human spirit and ordinary people's remarkable ability to show compassion at the worst of times.

I made real friends on the street, with the people who, in my opinion, form the backbone of South Africa, the *heart*.

I connected with people on a human level.

Whenever I think of them I reconnect with my own humanity— the absolute treasure of the Universe.

The desire grew from deep within me to encourage and empower, to awaken in others what the people I had met had awakened in me—the desire to keep searching for my humanity in every corner of my life.

I am still learning to walk in what I can only describe as this "enlightened" state. What a wise woman Hilda was. "Enlightenment", according to Hilda, is the ability to expand our capacity to grow.

It is not that my life is now easy and free of self-doubt—I am human, after all—but what is exciting about my life now, is my desire to push past my own limitations and watch and engage with those who push past theirs, to overcome my prejudices and then use what I learn creatively.

You have probably guessed, I have never written a book in my life, but now that I have, I intend to develop this new found skill.

I even took myself to the Met film school in London and learned the art of film-making in a class full of young, seriously computer-literate film-makers!

I will write more, I will make movies, I will act, but only in projects that make me happy, and I will wake up every day asking myself how I can turn the light on in another person who may be stuck in the dark recesses of their own mind.

Come to think of it, if Farai was still alive, I wouldn't be his wife, maybe not even his friend, but I know I would attempt to encourage him to find the light.

I honestly believe that every single one of us has a purpose and has every right to be here.

I look forward to seeing the possibilities that lie ahead and further look forward to being the architect of my own destiny, the Michelangelo of my very own Sistine chapel.

I love South Africa and will, from wherever I am, work tirelessly for her salvation.

I found that law I had asked Jesus to show me through my sister, Sheila. When I could finally bring myself to speak to her, she introduced me to Buddhism. This law even has a name. It's called The Mystic Law.

I now dance to the beat of the drum, and I dream the dreams of the sangomas, the seekers of truth on the fiery continent of Africa, every single waking and sleeping moment of my life. I shall be dancing to it on my deathbed.

Acknowledgements

I would like to say thank you from the deepest part of my being to the ordinary men and woman that gave me their time and support when I was living on in the streets of Johannesburg. I am forever indebted to the men and woman who took care of me at the Brightwater Commons petrol station when I used their premises as a shelter. Thank you to the gentlemen who bought my car and taught me to keep an open mind. Thank you to my dear friends at SGI UK who never stop believing in me.

I would like to express my deepest gratitude to my close friend Nicholas Beveney for his continuous support and encouragement.

Thank you to James Woodhouse of Kwela books, for his perseverance and faith in this project .

Finally, I would like to say thank you to Lebo Mashile for her praise and support, having read the earlier drafts of this book.